Workbook for The Body Keeps the Score

Brain, Mind and Body in The Healing of Trauma.
A Path to Recovery

Dorian Marshman

TABLE OF CONTENTS

INTRODUCTION
Trauma and Recovery

Traumatic Experiences

Experiencing trauma is unfortunately a part of our lives; it can happen to any of us. Traumatic experiences or events are incidents that cause physical, emotional or psychological damage to a person. The type of traumatic experiences you could encounter in your life can vary from having an alcoholic parent or carer to emotional or physical abuse or even sexual assault. The list of what could potentially cause trauma is extremely vast, even the reactions to the events differ from person to person. These reactions are, in part, how our body and mind try to heal and recover. The behavioural manifestations of the brain and nervous system changes during these experiences and you can do a lot to help deal with and recover from such incidents when you have the tools to do so.

Traumatic events, when experienced in life, are potential causes distress and increased level of cognitive, physical, psychological, and emotional anxiety. Because of this, your day-to-day life is affected and disrupted.

Causes	Consequences
Natural Disasters, Death, Witnessing a bad scene (WAR VETERANS), rape, physical violence etc.	Anxiety, numbness, dissociation, exhaustion, depression etc.

The way you react to trauma depends on many things, such as the type and severity of traumatic events and the amount of support you have following the incident. It also includes other stressors currently being experienced in the person's life, certain personality traits, natural levels of resilience, and whether the person has had any traumatic experiences before. Common reactions include a range of mental, emotional, physical, and behavioural responses. These reactions are expected, and, in most cases, they subside as a part of the body's natural healing and recovery process.

We all respond to trauma in different ways, and the way a person reacts depends on many factors. Some of these factors include the severity of such a traumatic event, the support you receive from friends and families, and other types of trauma incidents you experience by the person at that same time.

It is also important to note that some common reactions are attributed to how people react during trauma. Examples of these reactions include feeling that you are being watched to check if other things might happen, constant situations of being in shock, getting upset, and a quick display of emotion. Others include becoming numb emotionally, constantly feeling exhausted, anxious, stressed, fatigue feelings, continually battling with fear and doing many things because of this fear, and finally, always being protective of the people closest you, especially your friends and families.

There are different ways the brain responds explicitly to trauma, and they can either be cognitive, physical, or emotional.

Mental and cognitive reactions to incidents and trauma include having a decreased memory and concentration, interfering and invasive talks about the trauma incidents, constantly replaying the incident in your mind repeatedly, and finally being in a state of abject disorientation and unrest.

Emotional reactions to incidents of trauma include fear, distress, panic, confusion, and anxiety. It may also consist of awe and shock, a numb feeling, withdrawal from people around you, emotional exhaustion, depression, hypersensitivity, and guilt. They include fatigue, distorted sleep, nausea, exhaustion, vomiting, headache, excess sweating, dizziness, and intensified heartbeat rate.

Due to all these above factors, there are some resulting behavioural reactions to these incidents of trauma. They include the avoidance of incidents that would make you remember the trauma incident, inability to stop thinking, acting or still concentrating on the traumatic incident that happened, losing your appetite or becoming extremely hungry, relaxed while tending towards activities of drug and substance abuse and sleeping disorders.

After going through a traumatic experience, it is expected that you are try to make sense of the whole event. You think and reflect on the reason it had to happen, how the entire incident occurred, how you were involved in the incident, and why you were involved in the incident. You may also think of why you experience the feelings you went through, how the trauma incident now reflects who you are and how the trauma has impacted your life.

There are some healthy ways to help reduce the burden of all reactions to a trauma event, and they include:

- Accepting your trauma experience and understanding that your reaction to it is to be expected

- Always assure yourself that you will get past it

- Try not to be overly frustrated or angry with yourself when you realise that you are not a hundred per cent efficient as you used to be before the train incident took place

- Understanding that alcohol and drugs are not and will never solve traumatic incidents. They only provide a slight good feeling, and the next minute, your problems are still there staring at you

- If possible, ensure that you aren't making any big or life decisions at that moment. Put them off until you get much better to make good decisions.

- Don't try to prevent your reactions to the incident like it never happened. Accept that it happened, feel the pain, and gradually move past it.

- Do not keep everything you feel to yourself, bottling your feelings will only make you angry all the time. Talk to someone you trust about it. Attend meetings and seminars on trauma and share your experience. See a counsellor or a physiotherapist. These little acts will go a long way for you.

- Stay busy and try to resume back to your typical day-to-day routine.

- Always set time to rest. Getting busy might make you have an overly tight schedule. Be careful with this and always ensure you rest.

- Always speak out about what you need. Talk to your parents, siblings, or guardian about anything you need.

- Exercise regularly. It is more than the regular strains you feel in your muscle. This is because exercise is a way of soothing your body, mind, and inner soul.

- Relax a lot. Some relaxation techniques include listening to music, following your hobbies, breathing exercises, going to the cinema or comedy shows, meditation and yoga.

- Please talk about your feelings or write them down.

- Confront your memory anytime you remember your trauma incident.

To properly heal and recover from any trauma, you first have to realise that any incident that poses a serious threat to your well-being, or that of others, causes the human body to move into a state of intensified arousal. You adopt the 'emergency mode' that leads to your inner alarms being triggered. The emergency mode allows an individual to use a ton of energy in a quick interval to maximise the likelihood of survival. Most people dwell in emergency mode for a brief time or until the unexpected danger has finished. Nonetheless, existing in emergency mode consumes a lot of essential power supplies. This is the reason people always feel very weak, tired, and exhausted afterwards.

The routine healing and recovery process involves the body coming down out of a state of heightened arousal. The internal alarms turn off, the high levels of energy subside, and the body resets itself to a normal state of balance and equilibrium. Typically, this should occur within approximately one month of the event.

Usually, when the body is undergoing healing and recovery from any traumatic incident, the body experiences a reduction in arousal degrees. It implies that the alarm is off, and therefore, the high level of energy usage is reduced. The body reacts by resetting itself to the normal state of the body. At this stage, the body strikes an equilibrium and balance. Healthily, this should be experienced after a month when the trauma incident happens.

It is also vital that you seek the help of a medical practitioner throughout this event. It would help if you didn't wait till the matter gets out of hand. You should seek these health practitioners when you notice you cannot effectively handle deep emotions or sensations and physical feelings. Also, if you cease to have feelings, continually feel empty even after a month of the incident, experience continual physical stress and numbness, experience nightmares and distorted sleep, or find that you cannot correctly handle relations healthily again, see the doctor as soon as possible.

After experiencing trauma and its effects, as we have explained above, it is possible that you are still battling with all these reactions and even experiencing worse after a month or more. At this stage, such a person has post-traumatic stress disorder (PTSD). This is because of prolonged experienced responses, which might lead to a lot of other things. Relationships with family and friends could be put under strain and slowly, the capacity to perform any work. In this situation, continuous stress leads to a higher stress level than we have explained above.

Recovery is also a process that has to be embraced by a trauma survivor before it can be felt. Survivors must be ready to put in all the work required. As we will discuss further in this book, having a high sense of responsibility is also essential. When the survivor efficiently manages the situation and takes responsibility, the actual healing and recovery process starts. This recovery steadily continues until the survivor finally gets over it.

Chapter One
DETECTING TRAUMA

EMOTIONAL AND PHYSIOLOGICAL TRAUMA: WHAT IS TRAUMA?

Definition

Psychological Trauma is a series of events that takes place but appears to be highly stressful. It can cause a whole variety of emotional and physical symptoms. It is worthy to note that not everybody that experiences a stressful event is likely to develop trauma. Trauma comes with different signs, which can either be short-lived or long-lived. Trauma can also be best described as an emotional feedback to horrible occurrences like natural catastrophes, accidents, or rapes.

A trauma-stressed person can feel the emotional effect immediately after the occurrence or later on, with long term—feelings of shock, and helplessness. In addition, physical symptoms can also set in. If it is a short-term trauma shock, the person affected starts recovering from time to time until total recovery is confirmed. If, after time, the severity hasn't decreased, the person involved could be experiencing PTSD, which is an actual mental disorder.

Types of Trauma

Acute Trauma

It is caused by only one stressful event. This type of trauma is an anxiety disorder that develops shortly after a traumatic event. It might be a matter of days, but any anxiety or stress you feel shortly after a traumatic event is a trauma. It is abbreviated as ASD. It usually lasts for about three days and sometimes lingers on till about a month after. Sometimes, it occurs within a month and is accompanied by symptoms similar to symptoms felt during post-traumatic stress disorder.

Acute stress disorder is caused by witnessing and experiencing one type of traumatic event, even if it occurs more than once. Insecure feelings of stress, extreme fear, intense horror, and helplessness are usually created. Some of the traumatic occurrences that can lead to acute stress disorder include:

- Death news, especially those of people close to you

- Death threats, whether it is directly attached or indirectly attached to people close to a person

- Serious trauma threats are instantly made to one or indirectly caused to people around us

- Threats to one's public image and integrity, whether directly to one or indirectly to another person close to one

It has been researched and confirmed that most people who go through traumatic events develop acute stress disorder. It is worthy to note that anybody who has passed through a traumatic event can develop acute stress disorder. But here are the examples of people who have a higher chance of experiencing it;

- People who have been directly affected by trauma incidents in the past

- People who have a record of Post Trauma Stress Disorder, or people who have once battled with acute stress disorder before

- People who have once dealt with or people who are dealing with mental disorders

- People who have once experienced dissociative symptoms when they face a traumatic event

The prevalent symptoms of acute stress disorder include:

- Dissociative symptoms, which include numb, detached, and insecure feelings. For emotional matters, you are unresponsive to it.

- Your surroundings or whatever is happening around you don't matter to you anymore. You develop a deceased awareness of your immediate environment.

- Your surroundings seem unreal and strange to you. This leads to realisation.

- It is a common cause of depersonalisation. It feels like your emotions aren't yours, and they don't belong to you.

- Occurrence of dissociative amnesia. It occurs because of a short-term memory activation that makes you forget the vital aspect and points of the traumatic event.

- Mental replay and recurrence of the traumatic incident.

- Persistence replays of the traumatic event via flashbacks, recurring images, illusions, thoughts, imagination, and illusions of the traumatic incident.

- Re-experiencing the trauma incident makes it feel as though you are reliving the event that led to the traumatic stress.

- Distress and uneasy feeling when you remember the incidents of that traumatic event or something related to the traumatic incident.

Diagnosis of acute dress disorder

The doctor's mental healthcare worker will ask some questions about the traumatic incident and your symptoms to get a good diagnosis. They have to be sure that these are not symptoms caused by other reasons aside from acute stress disorder. Some of these other causes might include:

- After-effects of drug abuse,

- Effects of other types of psychiatric disorder other than acute stress disorder

- Side effects of drugs or any type of medication

- Various types of health problems

Treatment of acute stress disorder

There are many ways of treating acute stress disorders, but these are a few common ways.

- Hypnotherapy

- Cognitive behavioural therapy fasts track the rate of recovery. This will also help to curb acute stress disorder earlier before it develops and turns to PTSD.

- They are subjecting one to exposure-based therapies.

- Acute stress disorder Symptoms are relieving medications. Examples of these are antidepressants, anti-anxiety medications, and SSRIs (Selective Serotonin reuptake inhibitors).

- It means to teach one about one's disorder through psychiatric education.

- The determination of one's real needs through a series of psychiatric evaluation

- Offering help in food, shelter, clothes, etc. Service bits are also granted if it is essential to help one locate and reconnect with one's facilities.

- If it is detected that one is prone to suicidal thoughts or attempts, such a person is hospitalised and held back. If it is also noticed that one has the propensity to learn others, hospitalisation is also resorted to.

It has been found that many people who have been diagnosed with acute stress syndrome end up later being diagnosed with PTSD. The PTSD test is usually done when the acute syndrome disorder persists even after a month when it is supposed to have disappeared. It is straightforward to detect this as a strong case of stress, and a wide range of complex functioning is seen. When treated early enough, chances of later developing PTSD reduce. Most times, PTSD cases are resolved. It is done within six months, and other times, it keeps on being experienced for up to a year or even more.

Is acute stress disorder preventable?

Since it is never a certainty that one spends time in this world without going through traumatic experiences, it might be challenging to say that acute stress disorder is preventable. Nonetheless, there are so many things to put in place to decrease one's chance of experiencing acute stress disorders.

It is, however, advised to seek medical help within a few hours of going through a traumatic experience. This will help one reduce the chances of developing acute stress disorder. Sine folks work in areas where traumatic stress is very high, and they should constantly engage in tasks that aid their preparation. Also, from time to time, counselling is advised. Preparation training includes some untrue enactment of traumatic situations and counselling that aids the strength of mooing mechanisms. This helps then decrease cases of acute stress disorder and PTSD, especially when a traumatic incident surfaces.

Chronic Trauma

This is because of a repeated and extended susceptibility to this horrible event. An excellent example of this includes bullying, child abuse, or cases of domestic violence. People often mistake and interchangeably use complex Trauma. Even though they share some similarities, they still differ from each other. One significant difference is that chronic trauma can be referred to as PTSD, but complex Trauma is even more severe than this. It is known as complex PTSD or simply C-PTSD.

The nervous system and trauma

During a very threatening incident, especially incidents that put your life at risk, whether imagined or real, the nervous system immediately switches to survival mode. The use of nerve signals can explain this.

Here is what exactly happens. Some small signals originate in the amygdala and are identified in the brain by their small structures. These signals alert the brain to be prepared for mobilisation, whether it is fight or flight. If this threat cannot be avoided because of helplessness, the nervous system switches to the third response threat, identified as freezing. Some examples of cases where one can record helplessness are child abuse in the home, etc. There is a psychological and emotional shutting down in this freeze mode. It helps to deter the victim's psyche from being too overwhelmed.

Freeze mode possesses a functional characteristic of survival, but in cases of persistence, it becomes maladaptive. For chronic trauma survivors, there is continuous freezing of the nervous system to this threat incident.

Causes of chronic traumas

Unlike acute trauma that involves a trauma following just a single incident, chronic trauma is a trauma that is being experienced after going through a series of incidents. These incidents are repetitive. Most times, they involve common issues but are not limited to them. These incidents include;

- Continuous cases of child abuse

- Extended exposure to fights and war

- Prolonged cases of sexual abuse

- Lengthy cases of domestic violence

- Prolonged exposure to continue natural disasters

There are still other cases, but these are the few common ones. Chronic trauma survivors are usually subjected to prolonged treatment. It is because the resulting symptoms and pain can be severe and long-winded.

Chronic trauma symptoms

Unlike acute trauma, where symptoms only take weeks to manifest, chronic trauma can take several years to fully manifest. Maladaptive coping mechanisms are usually the ways by which chronic trauma survivors survive. These symptoms are generally distress-filled, leaving the survivor looking for ways to take some gentle actions against them. People suffering from chronic trauma are usually associated with this after-action:

- Substance abuse

- Addiction

- Denial

- Social withdrawal is a type of avoidance behaviours

- Rationalisation

All the symptoms associated with chronic trauma survivors are severe and destructive to the daily regulation of the human body. Together with maladaptive behaviours, chronic trauma survivors have a high likelihood of exhibiting the following traits.

- Continuous cases of flashbacks

- Nightmares

- The constant belief that they are under threat

- Misjudging people

- Misreading facial expressions

- Fatigue

- Low self-esteem

- Bad sleeping pattern

- Overreactions to things that are regular incidents

- Impaired memory

- Violent outbursts

- Distress

- Anxiety

- Confusion

- Depression

- Antisocial

When these symptoms are experienced, they can be self-perpetuating. It makes survivors look for other means to stay sane. Most times, the last resorts are not usually professional treatments. They include unhealthy and self-destroying resorts like

- Reckless driving

- Violence

- Unwholesome relationships

- Substance use

- Violence

- High-risk sex with multiple partners, etc.

Task 1

ARE YOU TRAUMATIZED?

AIM: The goal of this exercise is to help you identify a traumatic event you have gone through and how you have responded to it.

Instructions: Tick the appropriate space in response to the feeling or experience as found in the first column.

	YES	NO	Further Comment
Has any hurtful incident happened to you before?			
Do you feel bad because of it?			
Did you react physically to it? E.g. quick			

heartbeat, dizziness or excess fatigue.			
Did you find it difficult to sleep?			
Did your level of anger at the world increase?			
Did you cope well with other activities?			
Do you agree you are traumatized?			

Figure 1 – Are you traumatized?

Treatment of Chronic Trauma

Chronic trauma affects almost everything in one's life, and that includes the bliss that comes with the normalcy of living as a sane human (it is very stressful trying to look like a balanced human being when you are indeed dealing with a lot of mental and emotional issues that are making you internally imbalanced). Other areas that are possible to be affected include your performance in school and at work, interpersonal relationships with people, passion, motivation, love interest, etc.

Not only is your mental and physical well-being affected, but you are also prone to further physiological damage through the various self-destructive coping mechanisms delved into to stay sane. Emphasising cases of substance use disorder and addictions, PTSD primarily causes them as chronic traumas.

To successfully deal with cases of chronic trauma, voluntarily opting for medical treatments is advisable. Thanks to the ever-rising technology, treatments are now available, and this will assist survivors in getting back to their everyday lives and health. Some standard therapy of chronic trauma includes:

- EMDR, which is referred to as Eye Movement Desensitization and Reprocessing

- Somatic Experiencing

- Trauma-Focused Cognitive Behavioural Therapy abbreviated as TF CBT

- Medications and drugs

- Therapy sessions

Trauma has a very significant effect on the nervous system, especially the tendency of the nervous system to self-regulate itself. Once there is a healthy means for the nervous system to regulate itself, it becomes hard for chronic trauma cases to continue reoccurring for a long time. Therefore, these treatments are essential. Eye Movement Desensitization and Reprocessing and somatic experiencing enable survivors to achieve an improved regulation in their nervous system. It will, of course, positively impact their trauma history.

Medication, drugs, and CBT will help survivors heal from chronic trauma as well. It is done by decreasing the rate of trauma symptoms experienced by the survivor to increase the tolerance gauge of the survivor to distress.

It is also worthy to note that a robust support system is essential in recovering from chronic trauma. It is because trauma cases have a way of making you feel extraordinarily isolated. It almost feels like nobody cares. To ensure that loneliness isn't profoundly felt by people recovering, social support groups and people who have successfully dealt and battled with this situation are always advised to stay close to these survivors. It makes them feel heard, endorsed, and highly understood. The feeling of acceptance will always have a tremendous positive impact and help improve results from therapeutic sessions. In addition, the risk that such a person will still engage in maladaptive and high rush self-destructive behaviours will be reduced.

3. Complex Trauma

It results from exposure of a person to different cases of traumatic events. As described above, PTSD is a common distress disorder caused by a traumatic incident and experience. Compared to a complex trauma condition, it is a common condition. Complex post-traumatic stress disorder is abbreviated with CPTSD, and it is becoming widely known by health practitioners now. CPTSD happens because of repeated cases of different trauma incidents that keep on happening over a long period. Compared to chronic trauma, which invokes the repeated occurrence of just a trauma type, complex trauma shows the repeated acts of different traumatic incidents over a long-time frame.

The symptoms of complex trauma comprise the symptoms of chronic anxiety and PTSD plus some additional severe symptoms. These other features include:

- Presence of uncontrolled feelings because there is difficulty in regulating emotions. It might be as frequent as sadness and explosive anger.

- Emotional detachment. It is caused by consciousness change, and it can involve the feeling of body detachment. It might also make the survivor forget the traumatic event once in a while.

- Personal guilt shaming. It might even make the survivor develop a deep negative subjective perception.

If you are suffering from these symptoms, you are prone to bad interpersonal relationships, whether with family, friends, colleagues, or even society at large. There are some severe cases where a survivor feels better associating and demanding relationships with people who would cause them harm. It is because that feeling and association feel very familiar to them.

It is worthy to note that the symptoms of PTSD and CPTSD are experienced differently in people. Even with one person, symptoms can continually vary. Therefore, it is always essential for family and friends or health workers associated with someone experiencing PTSD to constantly keep in mind that their beliefs and thoughts will not regularly talk about what they do or how they feel. A complex trauma survivor could also crave a close connection to their abusers, or seek abusive relationships. This kind of trauma bonding is not uncommon, especially for those who experience abuse of some kind from an early age.

What are the causes of CPTSD?

Different ongoing research is aimed at detecting how complex Trauma affects the brain. Nonetheless, some studies have been made on animals. It has been found out that traumas have long-lasting effects and consequences, especially on areas like the amygdala, prefrontal cortex, and hippocampus. These brain parts play a huge role in memory functioning and how humans respond to stressful circumstances. Any trauma that takes place for a long time, especially over many months or even years, has every possibility to result in complex trauma. Its common occurrence is seen in people who are abused by people who are supposed to protect and take care of them. Common examples include:

- Child trafficking

- Sexual abuse by a family member

- Different emotional and physical abuse

- Slaves or war prisoners

- Being in a war region for a long time

- Maltreatment or child neglect

The risk factors of CPTSD include:

- Severe cases of anxiety and depression or a family history of these conditions. An underlying mental sickness can also cause these.

- Development of temperament, which is best described as an inherited attitude trait.

- Mode of hormonal and neurochemical brain regulation. It is most essential in the brain's response to stress.

- Unhealthy lifestyle, especially not owning a home support system. It can also be seen as having a dangerous job.

How is complex post-traumatic stress disorder diagnosed?

CPTSD is a new condition that is still undergoing a lot of research work and studies. Many health practitioners are not aware of it yet. Because of this, it might be challenging to get an official treatment and diagnosis from health institutions. It is even possible that instead of diagnosing one with PSTD, CTPSD is confirmed instead, since the former is not a commonly known condition yet. As of now, there is no official rest that will help determine whether one has PTSD. But, all hope is not lost, it is advisable to keep the details of your symptoms and continually share them with your doctor. This will aid your doctor in ensuring a very accurate diagnosis. Try to record when these symptoms started and any changes that have been recorded.

During your time with your doctor, describe all traumatic events that you have experienced in the past, plus all your written records of symptoms that you have felt.

It is also possible that you may be asked about the history of mental issues in your family, including other liable risk factors. Be sure to open up and start honestly as well. If you have been relying on some types of drugs, medications, supplements, or any recreational drug, do well to inform your doctor. When you give accurate information and accurate medication recommendations that will go a long way in your healing process.

If you feel uneasy seeing your doctor for the first time, that isn't an issue. It is usual for people experiencing PTSD and CPTSD. You might need to meet with a couple of doctors before deciding which you will be more comfortable discussing with.

Vicarious Trauma

Vicarious transformation is the changes that occur in a trauma health worker or caregiver because of the empathic association between the trauma client and the caregiver. This happens because the caregiver handles the first-hand information of traumatic experiences related to them by trauma clients. Their job as a traumatic health giver is rewarding, but it can be challenging, especially the highly emotional people. Vicarious trauma isn't limited to trauma health givers only; it can also be experienced by people who have been frequently exposed to other people's traumatic experiences. When there is continual exposure, the belief system can be tampered with because of the news heard. Vicarious trauma is a trauma type that builds up; it results in the disturbance and makeup of a person's spiritual virtue. Other affected people include trauma survivors' assistants, first responders to trauma clients, social workers in the front line of helping trauma clients, journalists, first-hand health personnel, and humanitarian workers.

The symptoms are almost the same as the symptoms experienced during actual trauma. Only that this time, the causative event isn't a direct traumatic experience, but an emotional connection between those who experienced the traumatic event at first hand, plus these helping professionals. These emotional connections lead to outward distress, mood swings, sadness, irritability, and grief. There are recorded cases of social withdrawal, aggression, and violence.

The symptoms of vicarious trauma include:

- Intrusive thoughts concerning the situations of their clients

- Feeling of frustration, irritability, plus emotions of fear and anxiety.

- They are always deep in thoughts

- They experience distorted sleep and nightmares as well.

- Difficulties in identifying and managing boundaries with other people.

- Overly high and extreme sense of responsibility. It occurs in a way that one might even start thinking of doing too much than your role and responsibility requires.

- Fear of leaving work at the close of each day. It all starts when you notice you can't leave your workplace on time as expected.

- There is no burning connection, both with one's self and with other people as well. This will lead to a situation where there is a total loss of your identity.

- Wanting to spend time alone and withdrawing from the world and people

- Always wanting to be in control of everything, especially others, events, and outcomes.

These signs and symptoms are different, and it depends on the individual embodying them.

The effects of vacation traumatisation on workers are being looked into in different ways. One way is by creating policies and rules that will be of great advantage to their staff's well-being. For every form of dealing with vicarious trauma, some constant things determine the success of each approach. These continuous factors include connection rate, individual balance, and general awareness. A set of techniques involves the adaptation of coping strategies. These strategies include the incorporation of playtime, self-care, rest, and escape. Another type of approach is the transforming strategy. Transforming techniques help workers set up a healthy community that will help them find meaning and fulfilment through their work.

Various researches have also shown that a simple act of kindness and other show of virtues help to increase happiness and decrease the impact of vicarious traumas. Socially connected people seem to be less affected. Also, showing gratitude with a conscious effort increases the satisfaction of these workers as well, thereby reducing the effect of vicarious trauma. In addition, acts aimed at self-care will go a long way. Practices like meditation, yoga, exercises, and music are beneficial to those who practice them.

Vicarious trauma operates on a mechanism of empathy and self-care. The rate at which this empathy affects individuals varies depending on the experiences each person has had to go through. However, one thing has been identified, and these would go a long way to curb vicarious trauma. Workers must stop putting themselves in the shoes of trauma clients. It makes them prone to feelings of sadness, worry, frustration, and distress. Instead, if they can only imagine what these trauma survivors went through doing no self-attachment, they might feel extra kindness and be moved to support survivors.

Some important tips that will go a long way in looking into symptoms of vicarious trauma include:

- Reaching out to people that can help. Now, many services cater to the ability of people to discuss their problems with an online doctor that you do not know or have never met before. If not, you can contact a trusted friend, counsellor, or anybody you are sure will listen well to you and devise a means out.

- Engage physically and mentally with tasks that will boost your emotions positively. Some of these include reading a book, going to the cinema, taking days off work for the essence of stability, seeing your friends, and going for picnics, rides, and walks as well.

- Take enough rest. The importance of rest can never be overestimated. Just some days off might want you only need

- Play and drink of water. Have fun doing all your hobbies. Opt for things that interest you and make your path as well.

Secondary Trauma

This form of trauma results from a close association with someone who has gone through a traumatic experience. This type of trauma can be contracted by mental health workers and family members of a trauma patient. It is most common when that patient has PTSD.

Secondary trauma is mostly mistaken with compassion fatigue, job burnout, the second victim syndrome, and vicarious trauma. There might be some shared meaning and concepts, but they are all different phenomena.

Compassion fatigue can be best described as the decreased efficiency of health care personnel to function very well because of the exposure and contact with the distressed feelings and sufferings of the patients they are taking care of. It is a natural feeling that plays out when health care professionals learn about their patient's traumatic experiences. Both are often used interchangeably, but the difference is that secondary trauma is limited to only workers who take care of trauma clients. Compassionate fatigue is used and not limited to trauma cases only. Instead, it cuts across to every person who specialises in giving treatment to other people.

The difference between secondary and vicarious trauma is the inner change and experiences of health care or other people prone to vicarious trauma, as described in the vicarious trauma section. It results from empathy and emotional connection felt because of direct engagement with the experiences went through by trauma survivors. This direct contact with their experiences results in a change in the mental makeup of such a person. Unlike other similar concepts, vicarious trauma is the most identical to secondary trauma. The difference between them is that vicarious trauma shows just a subtype feature of post-trauma stress disorder and negative alterations in the beliefs and emotions of such a person. It is limited to this, as vicarious trauma does not address other aspects of post-trauma stress disorders symptoms like hyperarousal, re-experiencing, etc.

Second victim syndrome, abbreviated as SVC, is used to describe the essence of a medical mistake on health care providers, especially when the health care provider feels responsible for the outcome for any medical error made. Patients and health care receivers are the victims of medical mistakes made, but health care professionals are affected negatively by these medical errors, too. They can be best described as the second victims, after the patients.

Job burnout, the last similar concept to secondary trauma, is the distress health workers feel due to accumulated stress and lack of fulfilment at one's workplace. Job burnout is a potential sign and symptom of secondary trauma stress, but secondary trauma stress is not a symptom of job burnout. Burnouts have nothing to do with traumatic events and post-trauma stress disorder.

Chapter Two

COMMON SIGNS AND SYMPTOMS OF TRAUMA

- Signs and Symptoms of Trauma

- Causes of Trauma and Consequences of Trauma

- Diagnosis and treatment of Trauma

SYMPTOMS OF TRAUMA

All the signs and symptoms of trauma fall into either the mild category or the severe category. Whether it is going to be harsh or gentle depending on the following categories:

- The person's background is a crucial factor, as it affects and determines how they approach and handle all matters, including emotions, as this includes Trauma and PTSD.

- What the trauma event entails

- How much trauma a person has witnessed before

- Absence or presence of any other type of mental health disorder

- The behavioural pattern of such a person

Task 2

ARE YOU TRAUMATIZED?

AIM: The goal of this exercise is to help you identify the key pointers to trauma events and victims.

Instructions: Tick the appropriate space in response to the feeling or experience as found in the first column.

Have you experienced?	YES	NO	Further Comment
Loss of Interest in your hobbies			
Anxiety			
Denial of hurtful memories			
Recurrent Nightmares			
Withdrawal from activities/people			
Numbness			
Insomnia			

Treatment of PTSD and Substance Use

PTSD and substance use is the typical resort of trauma stressed individuals. These people believe substance use is the only way to help them regulate their emotions back to normal. While it is pretty accurate that substance use can help alter moods and emotions, it doesn't do stabilisation. Aside from the fact that it just changes one's perspective, this effect isn't permanent. The quest to keep up with this temporal mood alteration leads to substance use disorder. PTSD occurs because of a very severe shock or trauma. Its effects and symptoms are pretty intense, and therefore its treatment isn't taken mildly. It doesn't end there.

Because the healing process has been distorted, the time frame of healing continues to get longer while complicating the patient's capability to attain success in almost all these different life aspects.

Significant harmful substance use is masking all symptoms of traumatic stress in the patients. These symptoms need to be appropriately evaluated and treated for the sake of recovery. Nevertheless, the moment a factor masks it up, they appear absent with a pretence that nothing needs to be treated. Thereby causing harm to the patient's recovery process.

It is also possible that substance use disorders can make the doctor or counsellor in charge of treatment misinterpret trauma stress symptoms.

Stages of recovery from trauma

Stage 1: Safety, stability and dealing with Deregulation

The feelings of safety and stability have to be reinstated into the sentiments of a trauma client, and this is the major first step. This is because trauma patients are not comfortable in their skin and in any relationship they find themselves in. They do not feel safe about anything anymore. To help them recover this safety and stabilisation, a secure and reliable environment has to be built. It is not about getting the material things or providing them with money at this stage.

At this stage, the little things matter. Acts of kindness, care, love, being listened to, reassured that all is well, etc., will go a long way for them. This helps to provide them with an environment free from physical hurts and emotional regrets. An emotionally stable environment is achieved with this. These random acts of kindness also help them to properly manage any post-traumatic stress disorder that can still surface at that point. For example, cases of nightmares and flashbacks can be triggered by any action from others or events. But once the aim of this stage is achieved, it helps their body remain calm and leads to the soothing of their mind. Hence, the quality of their daily life keeps improving from time to time until a total recovery is achieved and the traumatic client does not relive the traumatic experience.

Stage Two: Remembrance, Mourning, and Coming to Terms with Traumatic Remembrances

In this stage of the recovery, the survivor needs to go through a grief process to help overcome their traumatic experience. The help of an experienced trauma worker is needed. It might be a psychologist or a trauma specialist, a counsellor, or any other health care professional at your disposal. Such personnel have enough information that will assist and speed up your healing process. In countries with commendable and functional international healthcare bodies, therapies like ESMR (Eye Movement Desensitization and Reprocessing) or CBT (Cognitive behavioural Therapies are commonly used.

At this stage, mourning and show of emotions occur. What is mourned are the losses caused by the trauma incident you have faced.

Stage Three: integrate and reconnect

At this third stage, you are now in possession of your identity you have created and possess a new sense of self. This is most clear in the way you redefine yourself and open yourself to new relationships and opportunities. The trauma is now part of your story, but it no longer controls your actions or defines who you are anymore. You embrace a new life, new purpose, new opportunities, and new meanings.

Please note that in these stages we have mentioned no rule strictly guides how one should heal. This implies that there is no wrong or a right way to heal. As long as you are healing and experiencing these traits, your healing is as valid as another person who did not cure the same way you did. A bonus tip is that throughout all these stages, you have to accept and embrace your feelings continually. Embracing your feelings makes you take your emotions and feelings in the best possible way, and once this is put in place, your hearing will play out and manifest more easily.

Stage Four: Posttraumatic Growth or PTG

After successfully going through these three stages above, the ending result is that you move into the post-traumatic growth stage. Once you get to this stage, it confirms that your healing process is genuine. Post-traumatic growth happens when you feel new and positively changed by your experience of distress and trauma. At this stage, positive and healthy psychological changes are recorded because of the traumatic experience that has been experienced. It automatically increases your level of functioning and raises you to a much higher psychological region.

This is clearer in almost all grateful people, not for the traumatic incident they went through, but for the pain they felt because of this traumatic experience. The pain they endured strengthened them and made them a better person than they used to be. Post-traumatic growth doesn't result in you getting your former life before the traumatic experience back; it is instead triggers mature change in you, especially regarding how you perceive the world. This has led to people opening foundations to help others, or human rights ambassadors and advocates to ensure that trauma and abused people have their own voice. At the same time, others have used their experience to keep checking on survivors and devise means of helping them have a relatively faster healing process.

Chapter Three

SCIENTIFIC AND MEDICAL FACTS ABOUT TRAUMA

NEUROFEEDBACK

Through talk treatment, patients might come to comprehend that they are at this point not at serious risk, yet may keep on encountering increased nervousness, frenzy, flashbacks and bad dreams.

This is because trauma influences something beyond our considerations. The trauma changes the cerebrum and body so that talking and thinking will most likely be unable to turn around. Recuperating from trauma requires mending the cerebrum and body's science, not simply our emotions.

Neurofeedback is one of the new encouraging, proof-based treatments that tend to the more profound, fundamental organic changes that result from trauma and PTSD. In this chapter, we address questions including:

- How does trauma influence the mind and body?

- What is neurofeedback treatment?

- Does neurofeedback assist with trauma?

- What kinds of neurofeedback are useful for trauma or PTSD?

Trauma Therapy: Talking probably won't be sufficient.

Talk treatment for trauma can be useful in numerous ways, including:

- Approving feelings and assisting patients with the understanding that they are not at fault for what occurred

- Taking a look at the horrendous accident through another focal point

- Giving a feeling being supported and cared for

Patients don't simply recollect what occurred as a lucid story – they additionally recall how they felt and how their bodies responded. They remember or re-live how frightened they were, just as their heart starts to pound and begin to have trouble relaxing.

Often enough, talk treatment can't address these recollections of trauma that have become imbued in the body's science.

Moreover, one investigation discovered that about 40% of patients with PTSD drop out from CBT (intellectual, social treatment), the most suggested kind of talk treatment for trauma. Patients need a more far-reaching sort of treatment with better results.

How does trauma influence the cerebrum and body?
How does trauma change the brain?

Trauma removes an individual's feeling of wellbeing and steadiness at a profound, centre level and initiates the amygdala, nervous tissue which is in charge of both our survival instincts and our emotions. Here, information is collected, and it is where fear can be detected. When we are affected by a traumatic event the amygdala detects fear and becomes overly active, creating an uncomfortable and stressful feeling, making it difficult to relax and even sleep.

Talk treatment works at the prefrontal cortex, where we plan, learn, and sort out. However, it doesn't convey too well with the limbic framework. As such, talk treatment can interest our feeling of thinking and language, yet it doesn't address the more profound pieces of the mind that experience and stores the recollections of trauma.

During a horrendous accident, the amygdala alarms the nerve centre, a piece of the mind that organizes the body's pressure reaction by delivering chemicals like cortisol. What's more, the autonomic sensory system - which controls our compulsory body capacities - goes into acute stress mode. This implies having a quicker pulse, breathing all the more shallowly, perspiring, and not having the option to think obviously.

Along these lines, trauma can change the body's science. Even after the trigger has gone, the amygdala can clutch the actual memory of trauma, and our bodies can stall out in this acute stress mode, leaving us with more elevated levels of cortisol and indications of hyperarousal.

New treatments for calming the brain and body after trauma

What is neurofeedback treatment?

Neurofeedback is a non-intrusive, proof-based treatment that can support better mind work through brainwave preparation.

Our synapses convey through electrical driving forces, otherwise called brainwaves. Ordinary brainwave examples can be disturbed by trauma. Neurofeedback can assist the cerebrum with becoming adaptable and foster better examples and reactions, a cycle known as neuroplasticity, bringing back calmness.

How does neurofeedback work?

At the point when a patient's brainwave action moves into a better expression, the mind is rewarded with wonderful videos and sounds. Our cerebrums, very much like creatures, are continually looking for rewards. During a solitary neurofeedback meeting, the cerebrum is offered various chances to self-address and be remunerated.

Since neurofeedback doesn't expect patients to discuss previous events, they can unwind and allow their cerebrums to accomplish the work. Nonetheless, patients must have an authorized psychological wellness supplier address if affiliations, sentiments, or recollections come up during or after the meeting.

Does neurofeedback treatment assist with trauma? What's the proof?

The objective of trauma centred neurofeedback is to help people shift from a hyper-stimulated state to a quieter one so they can encounter a feeling of wellbeing.

There have been many examinations showing that neurofeedback can assist with the side effects of PTSD. Some have even shown that neurofeedback can change the cerebrum capacity of PTSD patients on imaging or fMRI.

Moreover, the degree of indication improvement in the greater part of these examinations has been huge. Indeed, the impact size with neurofeedback in many investigations has been more noteworthy than any prescription utilized for PTSD.

One limit of flow research is that the quantity of individuals associated with each study has been generally low. Future examinations that are bigger and better-planned will give us more knowledge into the advantages of neurofeedback.

What kinds of neurofeedback treatments are useful for trauma or PTSD?

Neurofeedback is an umbrella term that alludes to a wide range of brainwave preparation. There are two sorts of neurofeedback that appear to be particularly useful for trauma patients dependent on clinical exploration:

- ILF (infra-low recurrence) Training for Trauma

What's going on here? This type of neurofeedback trains the slowest brain waves that are associated with directing the cerebrum's pressure reaction. If this reaction isn't as expected, the mind can be set off by even the slightest trigger.

What do patients encounter during a meeting? The objective of ILF treatment is to help the mind move to a less stimulated and quieter state. Patients frequently report feeling truly and genuinely more settled after these meetings. Exploration and clinical perceptions find that patients regularly experience an adjustment of their pulse, muscle strain, and skin temperature as they move out of acute stress mode into a more settled, more loosened up.

- Alpha-theta Training for Trauma

This sort of preparing empowers alpha and theta brainwave action, the two of which are related to contemplation and unwinding.

What do patients encounter during a meeting? At the point when patients have an expansion in both of these brainwaves, they can enter a covert government among alertness and rest. In this state, individuals are more open to handling things in a new and better manner.

After these meetings, patients might find that when they ponder previous occasions or injuries, they have more knowledge of their feelings without feeling crippled, upset, or overpowered.

Incorporating ILF and Alpha-Theta Treatment

Patients in our centre regularly do ILF treatment before alpha-theta preparation, permitting them to encounter a feeling of quiet and wellbeing prior to handling trauma. Despite the fact that patients are not needed to think or discuss their trauma, a few patients might find that recollections or affiliations come up during or after a meeting. Therefore, it is significant that an emotional well-being expert is available when patients are doing neurofeedback preparation.

New methods for Healing from Trauma

Patients who haven't improved with talk treatment shouldn't feel alone. Trauma is a staggering occasion that has long haul consequences for the mind and body. There are profound organic explanations behind why patients might require extra help or medicines.

During the last 15 years, I have explored and assessed various diverse trauma medicines. I would say neurofeedback stands apart as one of the most accommodating medicines for patients with trauma. Long stretches of examination and clinical experience of specialists support the capability of neurofeedback to help some more.

Kids are regularly seen as profoundly strong and ready to spring back from pretty much any circumstance; however, horrendous encounters in adolescence can have extreme and durable impacts well into adulthood in case they are left unsettled. Youth trauma can come about because of anything that causes a kid to feel powerless and disturbs their feeling of wellbeing and security, including sexual, physical or obnoxious attack; abusive behaviour at home; a shaky or hazardous climate; division from a parent; disregard; tormenting; genuine ailment; or meddlesome operations.

In case you're living with the mental results of a traumatic adolescence, there are six different ways to recuperate your youth trauma and recover your life that we will go into more detail with in later chapters along with simple exercises for you to carry out.

1. Recognize and see the truth about the trauma. Casualties of youth trauma regularly go through years, limiting the occasion or excusing it by imagining it didn't occur or by surrendering to sensations of culpability or self-fault. The main

way you can start recuperating is to recognize that an awful accident did happen and that you were not answerable for it.

2. Recover control. Sensations of powerlessness can convey into adulthood and can cause you to feel and carry on like an unending casualty, making you settle on decisions dependent on your past aggravation to the point when the past is in charge of your present.

3. Look for help, and don't seclude yourself. A characteristic intuition that numerous trauma survivors have is to pull away from others. However, this will just exacerbate the situation. A major piece of the recuperating system is associating with others, so put forth the attempt to keep up with your connections and look for help. Converse with a confided relative, companion or instructor and consider joining a care group for overcomers of youth trauma.

4. Deal with your wellbeing. Build up an everyday schedule that permits you to get a lot of rest, eat correctly and exercise consistently. Above all, avoid alcohol and medications. These might give impermanent alleviation yet build your sensations of sadness, uneasiness and detachment and can deteriorate your trauma side effects.

5. Gain proficiency with the genuine importance of acknowledgement and giving up. Acknowledging something doesn't mean you're saying it's ok. Acknowledgement implies you've chosen how you will manage it. You can choose to allow it to govern your life, or you can choose to release it. Giving up means permitting your awful recollections and sensations of a terrible youth to deny yourself a decent life now.

6. Supplant unfortunate quirks with great ones. Unfortunate quirks can take many structures, similar to antagonism and continually doubting others, or turning to liquor or medications when sentiments become too difficult to even think about bearing. Unfortunate quirks can be difficult to break, particularly when they're utilized as support to assist you with trying not to remember the aggravation and trauma of your youth. A care group or an advisor can assist you with learning the apparatuses important to end your unfortunate quirks and supplant them with great ones.

INHABITING YOUR BODY

Regularly after encountering trauma, the body can feel separated or even like the adversary, and reconnecting to it is terrifying. Being in your body was an agonizing spot to be in at the time of the trauma and after it, and it may have appeared to be more secure and important to detach from it. Your body may encounter torment or uneasiness because of past trauma, and it's simply natural to have an underlying inclination to keep away from that.

How to inhabit your body

To help you through, here are some different ways that your body can be a partner during trauma recuperation.

1. Comprehend Your Body's Response to Traumatic Experiences

The more you think about why your body and mind react to horrendous encounters and updates, the better your capacity to explore them.

Our minds are made of various parts that serve various capacities. At the point when our mind recognizes a danger, for example, a token of past trauma, the more seasoned, cruder piece of our cerebrum that behaves like a caution framework starts the reaction of battle, flight or freeze. When we are encountering that reaction, the thinking part of our mind is, as of now, not ready to work how it did before the traumatic experience.

We might wind up becoming suddenly angry at others or begin avoiding them. While these reactions can be unquestionably difficult, it doesn't imply that you are "broken" it is the cerebrum doing precisely what it has developed to do, to guard us in what it sees as dangerous circumstances.

When an individual has encountered trauma, the caution framework in the mind can become extremely touchy to apparent dangers and lead to these reactions happening significantly more habitually when there is no longer any danger.

When we can perceive this reaction is occurring, we can all the more viably deal with our subsequent contemplations, sentiments, and activities.

2. Ground Yourself with Your 5 Senses

Horrible recollections can manoeuvre you into the past, while nervousness and hypervigilance project dread into what's to come. If you connect with your body right now, you can get some separation from the contemplations that don't serve you. The present is the main spot where any of us can make the change.

You can ground yourself by checking out your environmental factors for objects attached to your five detects. Attempt to discover:

- Five unique things you can find in the room

- Four things you can touch

- Three things you can hear

- Two things you can smell,

- One thing you can taste.

Did you see anything you didn't previously? If you are going through a distressing event or discussing your trauma, have a go at holding an establishing object (a concern stone, beaded armband, or stress toy) or use a solid, satisfying aroma like a diffuser or fundamental oils. Zeroing in on the actual sensations while you talk can assist you with remaining clear and grounded.

3. Make Body Awareness

Listening to your body's sensations can assist you with acquiring a superior comprehension of your triggers, and give you a superior feeling of what instruments will be best.

Require a moment to check your body. Take stock of specific sensations that you're feeling:

- Are you holding any strain in your jaw, shoulders, or stomach?

- Does this strain develop when you are in distressing circumstances?

- Do you encounter continuous stomach issues or headaches?

These would all be significant messages that your body is reacting to your current or past circumstances. These sensations can be truly awkward and crippling occasionally; however, when you can figure out how to pay attention to them, you'll be in an improved situation to calm your body and your brain.

4. Associate with a Safe Person or Pet

While this may not be possible for everybody, safe contact like embracing or clasping hands with an individual you trust or stroking your pet dog or cat can be an extremely successful approach to control feelings.

5. Self-care

It is normally after encountering trauma to foster practices to adapt that can contrarily affect long haul wellbeing, such as confused eating, substance use, or taking part in other high-hazard practices.

Yoga, dance, and exercise have been found to help with mindset and well-being and be useful in trauma recuperation since they increment your capacity to move throughout conditions of incitement and unwinding.

In case you don't know where to begin, that is OK! Start slow.

Whatever you do, recollect that you don't have to go through this interaction alone. You didn't pick what befell you or how your body reacts to horrendous encounters. You can decide to find support, and it is here when you're prepared.

SELF-HEALING: START YOUR RECOVERY FROM TRAUMA

Awful experiences can happen to anybody. Each person who encounters trauma will react distinctively to the occasion or series of occasions. Every individual requires a treatment plan that is custom-made to accommodate their recuperation needs.

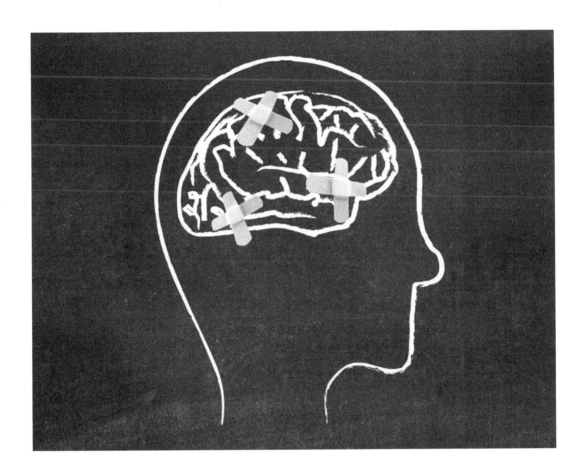

- Recuperating from trauma doesn't mean failing to remember your experience or not feeling any passionate aggravation when helped to remember the occasion. Recuperation implies becoming less upset and having more trust in your capacity to adapt over the long haul.

- Understand that you have experienced an extremely unpleasant experience or events, and it is normal to have a passionate response to it. Even though it's intense, you can manage it.

- Care for yourself by getting a lot of rest and exercise. Eat well. Physical and psychological wellness are firmly connected, so dealing with one will help the other.

- Scale back tea, espresso, chocolate, soda, and cigarettes.

- Attempt to try not to use medications or liquor to adapt, as they can prompt more issues in the long run.

- Set aside a few minutes for unwinding, regardless of whether it's paying attention to music or cleaning up–whatever works for you. It may be useful to become familiar with an unwinding strategy like reflection, yoga, reformist muscle unwinding, or breathing activities.

- Plan your days and attempt to plan some movement every day. Have a go at making a plan for every day, including some activity, some work, and some unwinding.

- Return to your ordinary daily schedule as quickly as time permits. However, relax. Try not to hurl yourself entirely into exercises or work, trying to avoid difficult recollections of the trauma. Tackle the things that should be done a smidgen at a time, and count every achievement.

- Try not to suppress your sentiments or square them out. Repeating considerations, dreams and flashbacks are unsavoury, yet they are normal and will diminish with time.

- Try not to settle on significant life choices like moving house or changing positions in the days and weeks after the horrible accident. Then again, make as many more modest, day by day choices as expected, for example, what you need to eat or a film you'd prefer to see. This can assist you with feeling more in charge of your life.

- Invest energy with individuals you care about, regardless of whether you prefer not to discuss your experience. Sometimes, you will need to be separated from everyone else, and that is okay, yet you should try not to spend too much time alone.

- Talk about your sentiments to somebody who will comprehend if you feel ready to do so. Talking things through is essential for the normal recuperating measure and will assist you with tolerating what has occurred. As you feel better, you might even wish to help other people who have experienced comparative circumstances.

- Allow yourself to rethink. A horrendous accident can influence how you see the world, your life, objectives, and connections. Once more, talking this through with others may help.

FILLING IN THE HOLES
Understanding the brain and body in trauma

Some parts of the brain are significant in seeing how the cerebrum and body work during trauma. They include the forebrain, the prefrontal cortex and the limbic framework, which is situated at the focal point of the mind, and the cerebrum stem.

When an individual encounters an awful accident, adrenaline hurries through the body, and the memory is engraved into the amygdala, which is essential for the limbic framework. The amygdala holds the information regarding the occasion, including the force and motivation of feeling.

For instance, in case you're on a thrill ride, your tactile data is "fear, speed, stress, energy, not perilous." The amygdala can capture the enthusiastic vibe of the occasion as it's a great ride which you'll be off shortly. The amygdala stores the visual pictures of trauma as tangible pieces, which implies the trauma memory isn't put away like a story, rather by how our five faculties were encountering the trauma when it was happening. The recollections are put away through visual pictures, smells, sounds, tastes, or contact sections.

Thus, after a real trauma, the mind can easily be triggered by tangible information perusing ordinary conditions as unsafe. For instance, a red light is not a red light; presently, it's a potential sparkle. A grill had been recently a grill, yet presently it seemed like a blast. The tangible parts are confused, and the cerebrum loses its capacity to segregate between what is compromising and what is typical.

The forward portion of our brain, known as the prefrontal cortex, is the same part where awareness lives, handling and thinking happens. When trauma happens, individuals go into a battle, flight, or freeze state, which can bring about the closing down of the prefrontal cortex. The cerebrum turns out to be fairly disarranged and overpowered because of the trauma. At the same time, the body goes into endurance mode and closes down the higher thinking and language designs of the brain. The consequence of the metabolic closure is a significant engraved pressure reaction.

Treatment approaches

Customary trauma treatments have been founded on the conviction that the ideal approach to address and recuperate PTSD side effects is to manage it in the "thinking" part of the mind through talk treatment.

Talking through the occasion was thought to assist an individual with understanding the trauma and gradually desensitize themselves to its force.

Over the last 18 years, cerebrum check innovation has permitted us to understand the contrast between what happens when individuals talk about past trauma and what happens when their body is re-encountering them. It has been discovered that discussion treatment endeavours to connect with parts of the mind that are "disconnected" and consequently can't resolve the trauma when individuals are in hyper-upset states.

Bessel van der Kolk, MD, a main specialist in the trauma field, says, "We've attempted to mend PTSD through talking and making the importance of the occasion, however, treatment strategies that assist with quieting excitement frameworks in the further locales of the cerebrum have been useful in quieting PTSD more than those that attempt to do through talking and thinking. We hit this 'base up preparing.'

Today we perceive that the front-facing piece of the mind has a restricted capacity to change, particularly when the body is in a trauma reaction or trouble. Talk treatment works when the mind is working; however, when the trauma memory commandeers the level-headed piece of the cerebrum, individuals may not hear words or think or make the importance of occasions and encounters. When the more deeply areas of the mind are in this condition of pain, survivors are back in the trauma, and their cerebrum and body appear to be in time travel.

Quieting the deeper regions of the brain

To calm those more profound areas of the mind, we start with "base up handling," using the sorts of treatment that will mitigate and calm the body. When somebody is in a started or hyperarousal state, we would prefer not to ask them trauma inquiries that can raise trouble and further engraving the trauma into the limbic framework. The aim for remedial meditations is to take oxygen and bloodstream back to the cerebrum to begin calming the body and getting to the higher districts of the mind.

Van Der Kolk resolves this issue by expressing, "Making a move is the centre issue. It's inaction that individuals reclaim their power and make mending, and words can't fill in for activity.

EMDR
There are various approaches to carry activity to the body and cerebrum. Today, one treatment choice that uses activity to immobilize the body and cerebrum is eye development, desensitization and reprocessing, or EMDR. EMDR uses reciprocal incitement to connect with the two sides of the mind in real life. Initially, this was finished by having an individual follow a specialist's finger back and forth before their vision field.

This respective development causes the horrendous memory circling in the passionate side of the cerebrum to incorporate with the intellectual part of the brain. The eye and mind development builds the capacity of the prefrontal cortex to "get on the web" or discover sanity in an awful accident.

SENSORIMOTOR THERAPY

Sensorimotor methods are additionally valuable in limbic quieting. In sensorimotor treatment, the specialist assists an individual with seeing tactile body reactions and being on top of their body's messages to address recuperating. It is a method for drawing in the body and the brain in the recuperation cycle.

Daniel Amen has recorded that individuals experience quieting in their limbic designs following EMDR treatment through his neuro-imaging studies. Different settings for limbic quieting incorporate mitigating music, supplication and contemplation, careful breathing, yoga, and exercise.

The accompanying basic exercises can support limbic quieting:

- Require 5 minutes toward the beginning of the day and evening to shake back and forth, or side to side, simply seeing and loosening up the body.

- Discover music or tones of music, with or without words that bring you into a condition of smoothness.

- Practice profound taking in groupings of three. For instance, inhale, inhale, and relax. Rest. Inhale, inhale, and relax. Rest....

- Take part in some type of activity for 12-15 minutes each day to build serotonin and dopamine.

- Take an interest in 5-10 minutes of the day of supplication or contemplation, as the profound focus of the mind is a region that can impact and quiet the more profound areas of the cerebrum.

Self-Responsibility

1	Do you feel like what happened was your fault?	YES/NO
2	Do you blame anyone else for what happened?	YES/NO
3	Do you think it is right to take responsibility for your recovery from what happened?	YES/NO
4	Do you understand that taking responsibility for your recovery from what happened does not mean you are at fault?	YES/NO
5	Do you understand that taking responsibility for your recovery from what happened does not mean other people did not have their role in what happened?	YES/NO
6	Are you willing to forget about others and focus more on yourself for the sake of your healing and recovery?	YES/NO
7	Are you willing to let go of this event so that it doesn't take over your life?	YES/NO
8	Are you convinced that the main cause of the issue is not what has happened but the aftermath?	YES/NO
9	Do you believe you are in charge of your life?	YES/NO

10	Are you ready to reach out and search for help?	YES/NO
11	Where will you start?	*****

Letting Go of The Past

1	Has there been a significant change in your daily life since the event?	YES/NO
2	Have you tried letting go of the past before?	YES/NO
3	Have you found yourself thinking excessively about the event in recent past?	YES/NO
4	Do you find yourself thinking so much about the past and trying to find out what could have been different?	YES/NO
5	Have you decided now to let go of the past and feel ready to do so?	YES/NO
6	Have you been trying to avoid the feelings that come from memories of the event?	YES/NO

7	Are you willing to practice mindfulness whenever you find yourself thinking about the event?	YES/NO
8	Are you willing to seek out help with letting go of the past?	YES/NO
9	Can you identify what type of therapy based help would be suitable for you?	YES/NO
10	Will you face the past without minimalizing it and just let go of it from now on?	YES/NO

Inhabiting your body

1	Have you been having problems with inhabiting your body since the event?	YES/NO
2	Have you been able to comprehend your body's response to the traumatic experience?	YES/NO
3	Do you find yourself being suddenly angry at others, staying away from them, or closing in on yourself?	YES/NO
4	Do you find yourself feeling extremely nervous or hypervigilant since the experience?	YES/NO
5	Will you endeavor to be more aware of sensations in your body from now on?	YES/NO

6	Are you willing to thaw when experiencing Flashbacks or Dissociation?	YES/NO
7	Do you have a safe person or pet you can associate with to deal with this traumatic experience by way of touch or comfort?	YES/NO
8	Will you make sure to deal with your body to increase resilience?	YES/NO
9	Are you ready to start slow and recollect that security consistently starts things out?	YES/NO
10	Do you believe that any solid shift you make is a stage toward recuperating?	YES/NO

Self-Healing

01	Do you understand that recuperating from trauma doesn't mean failing to remember your experience or not feeling any passionate aggravation when helped to remember the occasion?	YES/NO
2	Do you understand that recuperation implies becoming less upset and having more trust in your capacity to adapt over the long haul?	YES/NO

Workbook for The Body Keeps the Score

3	Are you able to perceive that you have experienced an amazingly unpleasant occasion, and it is normal to have a passionate response to it?	YES/NO
4	Are you willing to care for yourself by getting a lot of rest (regardless of whether you can't rest) and normal exercise?	YES/NO
5	Are you willing to scale back tea, espresso, chocolate, soda, and cigarettes?	YES/NO
6	Do you understand that you are to try avoiding the use of medications or liquor to adapt, as they can prompt more issues long haul?	YES/NO
7	Are you willing to set aside a few minutes for unwinding, regardless of whether it's paying attention to music or cleaning up (whatever works for you)?	YES/NO
8	Are you ready to invest energy with individuals you care about, regardless of whether you prefer not to discuss your experience?	YES/NO
9	Are you ready to talk about your sentiments to somebody who will comprehend if you feel ready to do so?	YES/NO
10	Are you ready to allow yourself to rethink and influence how you see the world, your life, objectives, and connections?	YES/NO

Filling in the Holes

1	Will you like to take active steps to work on your brain to aid quick healing from the traumatic experience?	YES/NO
2	Will you endeavor to take steps to accomplish the tasks below that will help with your decision above?	YES/NO
3	(A) Require 5 minutes toward the beginning of the day and evening to shake back and forth, or side to side, simply seeing and loosening up the body	YES/NO
4	(B) Discover music or tones of music, with or without words that bring you into a condition of smoothness	YES/NO
5	(C) Practice profound taking in breath in groupings of three. For instance, inhale, inhale, and relax. Rest. Inhale, inhale, and relax. Rest....	YES/NO
6	(D) Take part in some type of activity for 12-15 minutes each day to build serotonin and dopamine.	YES/NO
7	(E) Take an interest in 5-10 minutes of the day of supplication or contemplation, as the profound focus of the mind is a region that can impact and quiet the more profound areas of the cerebrum	YES/NO

8	Will you have an issue with any of the above listed five (5) steps?	YES/NO
9	Are you willing to work on any one you find a bit challenging?	YES/NO
10	Do you believe you can do it and let go of the past to have a normal and completely productive life?	YES/NO

Chapter Four

DOES TRAUMA END?

Does trauma end? Can one completely heal from trauma?

Overcoming trauma is not a simple process and is different for each person. It takes time to slowly leave the feelings of helplessness, numbness and disconnection behind you. Being able to live comfortably in the present without the negative thoughts and reminders acting as obstacles in your daily life, means that you are on the path to recovery.

Recovery from trauma is a personal process that everyone goes through differently. Healing from trauma happens differently in every person, all depending on certain factors. These factors include your beliefs and awareness of things, coping mechanisms, resilience and strength, access to supportive friends and family members, and the psychological functioning of your brain before the traumatic experience.

Getting past trauma and successful healing has to do with the tendency to live your present life without harbouring the thoughts of distress, fear and frustration when you flashback to feelings and thoughts that have happened in the past. It doesn't mean you have to forget the incident entirely. Recovery from trauma means that you have placed the past before you and are enjoying the present. Moreover, not letting any negative feelings ruin the present. This is a deliberate and continual process. This is a sign that the traumatic incident is not, in any way, controlling your emotions and life.

Trauma, whether psychological or emotional, usually occurs because of cases of abuse or unusually stressful incidents that tamper with your sense of self and feel like a threat to your safety or life. Traumatic experiences make it very hard for you to cope and play with your ability to integrate feelings and emotions.

You will certainly need time to be able to feel safe again. Nonetheless, it doesn't make it a hopeless situation. No matter what happens, you can always get your life back.

Antidepressants can work, but there is no magic pill, it definitely will not cure you alone. It takes constant work that we will talk about later and help you recover step by step using small bite-size tasks in the next chapters.

In the cases of antidepressants, they work on the hippocampus, which is the known organ that counteracts stress. Some researchers have been carried out on animals, and some phenomenon has been recorded. These phenomena work in the same way as human beings as well. One of these findings is that post-traumatic stress disorder clients usually have some organs in the brain become smaller than their normal sizes, which is only this way when they experience PTSD syndromes. These organs include the hippocampal, the prefrontal cingulate option, the anterior cingulate option, and the anterior cingulate function. While some of the organ sizes decrease, some other sizes increase, and an example is the amygdala. There is also an increase in the norepinephrine and cortisol responses to stress. But note that once a PTSD client recovers, these sizes return to their natural forms and sizes. Effective PTSD treatments have promoted neurogenesis, and this was found out during animal studies.

Neurobiology of PTSD

Post-traumatic stress disorder has some recognisable symptoms, including meddling thoughts, erratic responses, forgetfulness, memory changes, distorted sleep, concentration changes, intrusive thoughts, nightmares, distress, hyperarousal etc., as we have discussed in subsequent chapters. The result is that all discomfort and symptoms experienced during PTSD result from the stress-induced alterations in the brain's structural and functional processes. The symptoms are just behavioural and physical manifestations. Traumatic stress usually leads to changes in the neurochemical structures in some specific regions of the brain. The changes might result from chronic changes or acute changes.

This leads to the brain experiencing long term changes, especially the brain circuits, which are directly or indirectly involved in stress responses. Two different neurochemical systems are over important to stress response and they are cortisol and norepinephrine.

Some other systems play an important role in stress response, including the Hypothalamic-Pituitary-adrenal axis system and the corticotropin-releasing factor. They are otherwise referred to as the HPA system and the CRD system, respectively. The hypothalamus first releases the CRF through the stimulation of the ACTH that the pituitary releases. It results in the adrenal releasing glucocorticoid, which is the cortisol found in men. This has adverse feedback on the axis at the pituitary and hippocampus, sites of the central brain and the hypothalamus. One effect cortisol has is to facilitate survival. One such effect and role is to trigger the HPA axis. To trigger the HPA, CRF helps mediate certain behaviours related to fear and are also responsible for triggering various other neurochemical feedbacks to stress. For example, the noradrenergic structure through the stem locus coeruleus of the brain. Noradrenergic neurons discharge transmitters and spread it all over the brain; this is attributed to an upswing in warning and alertness behaviours, significant for withstanding with an acute warning.

Some research was carried out on animals, and it was detected that the HPA axis is usually affected by early stress. It has a long-lasting effect on this region and the norepinephrine as well. Some medical researchers have shown different memory function changes and brain circuits immediately after a traumatic incident—areas like the medial prefrontal cortex, hippocampus, and amygdala. The medial prefrontal cortex is the region that facilitates changes in memory, while the hippocampus is an area of the brain that is concerned with the memory's oral declarative. The hippocampus region is very sensitive to stress as well. In animals, the CA3 region located inside the hippocampus is the region responsible for stress. Once there is neuron damage in this region, stress sets in. This CA3 region is also moderated by neurogenesis inhibition, increased glutamate level, reduction in brain-derived neurotrophic factor, and hypercortisolemia. Depletion in fresh learning is also associated with the stress linked to increased levels of glucocorticoids.

When trauma clients use antidepressants, they help to curb the effects of stress by stimulating neurogenesis. Asides from antidepressants, other agents have been proven to curb hippocampal damages brought about by stress. Phenytoin blocks any damage caused to the hippocampus through the modulation of excitatory neurotoxicity caused majorly by amino acids. Tianeptine, fluoxetine and DHEA also have similar effects with phenytoin. These prescriptions may have a mutual mechanism of action via the upregulation of cyclic adenosine monophosphate response element-binding protein. Such medication consequences of trkB messenger ribonucleic acid and BDNF can lead to long-term impacts on the brain system and processes. There is recent proof that neurogenesis is vital for the behavioural impacts of antidepressants, although this remains to be a basis of discussion.

Deregulation that has accumulated over a long time on the HOA axis is connected with PTSD. The cortisol having a low level and the CRF having a high level are also associated with chronic PTSD. When you are exposed to something that reminds you of your trauma stress, there is cortisol release. Some other few studies have been made on neurology to test traumatised children. The rare research of the impacts of premature anxiety on neurobiology performed in clinical communities of traumatised youngsters has mainly been uniform with conclusions from animal research. Investigation in traumatised kids has been mixed up by cases associated with psychiatric diagnosis and examination of trauma. A handful of studies have not precisely explored psychiatric diagnosis. In contrast, various other experiments have focused on kids with trauma and depression and others with trauma and post-stress trauma disorder. Girls who have been sexually abused in which consequences of specific psychiatric diagnosis is caused by post-traumatic stress disorder exhibited heightened degrees of Cortisol assessed in urine that is only 24 hours old. Emotionally neglected youngsters from a selected orphanage had heightened Cortisol degrees over a diurnal interval as juxtaposed with other control research. Maltreated school-aged teenagers with clinical category internalising difficulties had heightened Cortisol levels as juxtaposed with other control experiments as well.

Depressed children that are yet to start schooling showed an increased level of cortisol reactivity to stress. Women who have experienced childhood abuse exhibited a heightened level of suppression to a low dose of cortisol. The measurement of the low dose was 0.5mg dexamethasone. Women who have experienced post-traumatic stress disorder because of childhood sexual abuse exhibited reduced baseline cortisol measured on a day's diurnal examination of the blood plasma. This set of people also showed an increased cortisol reaction to traumatic stressors than a cognitive stressor with a neutral characteristic. Also, it was detected that patients having PTSD once suffered from deadening of memory function when treated with synthetic cortisol, which is otherwise known as dexamethasone. Grown-up women suffering from recession and a past narrative of premature preadolescence abuse exhibited a raised Cortisol reaction to an aggravating mental challenge compared to other research controls carried out. These outcomes show long-term alterations in anxiety responsive networks.

During early growth, stress is correlated with intensified cortisol and norepinephrine sharp response. In contrast, resting cortisol may normally exist or in low quantity with adultness, but there will always be a boosted cortisol and norepinephrine reaction to stressors. Also, premature stress is related to changes as regards hippocampal morphology that would stay hidden until maturity, plus an enhanced amygdala role and reduced medial prefrontal objective.

Conclusively, traumatic stress has an extensive span of consequences on brain role and system, as adequately as on neuropsychological organs of memory. Brain regions affected in the post-traumatic stress reaction comprise the hippocampus, prefrontal cortex, and amygdala. Neurochemical structures, comprising cortisol and norepinephrine, have a very significant function in the stress reaction system. They also perform an important function in recollection, accentuating the crucial interplay between the remembrance organ and the post-traumatic stress disorder response system—preclinical research exhibits how stress influences these brain regions. Similarly, antidepressants have aftermaths of the hippocampus, which equalise the consequences of anxiety. Also, the development of nerve growth referred to as neurogenesis in the hippocampus might be prominent to the effectiveness of the antidepressants.

Research in post-traumatic stress disorder clients shows changes in brain regions involved in animal surveys, including the amygdala, neurochemical stress response systems, prefrontal cortex and hippocampus. This also includes the regions of cortisol and norepinephrine. Medications that are productive for post-traumatic stress disorder show the growth of neurogenesis in animal research. These medications also lead to enhanced memory plus a heightened hippocampal size in most traumatic stress disorder clients. Prospective researchers are required to examine neural means in therapy reactions in PTSD clients.

Chapter Five

STEPS TOWARDS RECOVERY

GETTING PAST TRAUMA-WITH STEP-BY-STEP TASKS

- Acceptance and processing

- Self-responsibility

- Mindfulness

- Letting go of the past

- Neurofeedback

- Inhabiting your body

- Self-confidence

ACCEPTANCE AND PROCESSING

Life after a traumatic event or events can be very challenging to say the least, accepting the trauma that you have been subject to is one of the first stepping stones to reach healing. Recovery is possible and so is getting your life back to "normal", this process takes determination and commitment. It is, however, a very tiny price to pay in order to get your life back and regain your freedom.

Acknowledging the pain you suffered or are still suffering is essential in order to move forward. When feelings regarding your traumatic event pop up, don't block them out but identify those emotions you are feeling without overthinking them, just observe them.

It is proven that writing about your trauma can be a tremendous help, especially as it aids acceptance of what you went through and what you may have lost and helps you process what you have been through. Keeping a dairy/journal, not only about you past traumatic events, but also about how you are feeling now and you daily struggles can significantly reduce your stress levels. Emotional writing has a strong effect on mental health, reducing the feeling of anxiety and depression and can result in better quality of sleep along with increased clarity and focus during the day.

TASK

You don't have to start with anything overwhelming, just dedicating 15 minutes of your whole day will be enough. It's important to decide the time of day to this and stick by it. The most common time of day would be at the end of your day, either after work or just before going to bed. You need to buy a dairy or workbook, which you will use solely for this purpose. Then simply sit down and set a timer for 15 minutes at your decided time of the day. Begin to write any sentences, words or notes that come up when you recall your traumatic moments; it's important to not overthink things.

Repeat this process every day until you feel ready to move on to the next step and begin writing about thoughts or upheavals that you went through during the day without overthinking it. It's important to remember that it doesn't matter if you feel that you are not a good writer, the important thing here is what you write and not how you do it. Things like grammar, punctuation and spelling are not to be worried about.

CREATING A COPING STRATEGY AND IDENTIFYING TRIGGERS

Unwanted emotions or memories, or even flashbacks can be a part of post traumatic events, it's important that we identify what these triggers are for us and work on a coping strategy to help live our "normal" everyday life.

The things that remind you of you experience, which then cause your mind and body to react, are called triggers.

Triggers may differ from person to person and there are many different things that can set off a reaction to your past traumatic event. They can be anything from a particular smell to seeing a person. Some of the other most common are:

- A particular day (a birthday, Christmas, an anniversary)

- A noise that takes you back to the horrific moment

- A movie or a tv programme

- A place that takes you back to a specific moment

- Looking at an object that reminds you of something that happened

- Hearing a song on the radio that brings back memories of that moment or period in your life

For some people, recognising their triggers isn't such a difficult task, whereas for others it will take time. Some triggers could seem obvious and others could be left unnoticed. In fact, many people who suffer from PTSD believe that their reactions come out of the blue, but that's not the case. By improving your awareness of your triggers, you can decrease the impact they have on you.

Task

A simple way to identify your triggers is to ask yourself these questions after having a reaction (you could even try to do the same exercise thinking back to past episodes)

- Where were you?

- Who were you with?

- What were you doing?

- How were you feeling?

- What kind of situation was it? (a meal, a birthday, a lecture, a walk in the park)

- What did you see?

Take notes of your answers and keep them safe. You will eventually be able to pint out your triggers.

Coping

Now you have identified your triggers you will already be able to feel an improvement. You can also try your best to avoid them, however it can be extremely difficult. Another way to reduce the symptoms of a trigger is to adopt a coping method.

There are many ways of coping with uncomfortable emotions and reactions that do not need the help of others. This type of method is called self-soothing and is something you can practice alone.

Tasks

Finding ways to cope with stress and anxiety doesn't have to be complicated, here are some simple things you can try to self-sooth in order to make your negative emotions, thoughts and feelings easier to tolerate without letting them escalate into more serious reactions:

- If you begin to feel upset or sad then try making yourself a warm tea to drink on your favourite sofa, maybe watching one of your preferred tv series. You could also run yourself a relaxing bubble bath. The feeling of water touching your skin can give you a quick relief. Other things you could try include (if in summer) simply sitting a safe place under the sun, feeling the heat of the sun's rays warm your body. Try some of these and see which one works best for you.

- If your body enters into alert mode and you begin to feel hypervigilant and sensitive to everything around you, then you should try something more energetic. Try a game of tennis, football, a quick run or a brisk walk. If this doesn't work for you then try the opposite, deep breathing and stillness.

In all cases, please keep repeating to yourself that this feeling is not permanent and will pass. Nothing lasts forever, it will stop.

SELF-RESPONSIBILITY

Taking responsibility helps towards healing from trauma. If you have ever lived through a traumatic experience then you'll know that it's easy and understandable to feel like a victim. If you are struggling to recover from any type of trauma, all you are thriving for is to feel "normal" again. However, this sensation of feeling as if you were a victim, gets in the way of the healing process and keeps you prisoner of a victim's mindset. This kind of mindset includes feeling helpless and sorry for yourself but at the same time have feelings of self-blame, which leads to a fragile situation of frustration, anxiousness and depression. Breaking free of this way of feeling and thinking is essential for you path towards feeling "normal" again. This can be achieved through taking responsibility for yourself.

Taking ownership or responsibility for recovery doesn't imply that everything that happened is your fault. Neither does it mean that you have to force yourself to believe that you are at fault. It simply means that you are taking responsibility of ensuring that this incident does not take control of your life. With this, you indirectly make a statement that you are in charge of your life.

Choosing not to be self-responsible or own up to self-ownership can be very detrimental. When you blame others for what happened to you, or feel sorry for yourself, it simply means you are transferring the ownership or responsibility of your attitude to another person. By doing this, you stop yourself from creating better solutions that will lead to your recovery. Taking responsibility doesn't imply that others involved in the incident do not hold the blame, only that this time, you are choosing to forget about them and focus more on yourself for the sake of your healing and recovery. Putting up with ownership of our healing implies that you are accepting the situations for what they stand for. The incident wasn't your fault, but it still happened. And with those that are battling with addiction, negative outcomes of not wanting to take self-responsibility and ownership can trigger alcohol, drug or substance use disorder.

To fully take responsibility, one of the first things to do is to identify the problem. When the problem is duly identified, you can properly analyze how you are affected by the event. Accusing others disempowers those who resort to that alternative. Accusing seizes your time and stamina to envision rewriting situations we cannot control. Unknowingly, when we dissipate our energy at accusing others, we lend others the energy to dictate what to do with our own lives. When we blame others, we assume that the world is a cruel and unjust place to live. The difficulties we can settle, nonetheless, are only the terrible incident incited and not the incident itself. There is absolutely nothing we can do about the past, but we can compose our future by taking responsibility for our present situations. For those recuperating from traumatic incidents, do not forget that you can't alter whatever incident that has happened to you. You can settle the emotions and handle the consequence the incident has given rise to in our lives. There is a possibility for transformation and restoration.

After leavening the act of self-responsibility and ownership, another key point to work on is how to empower yourself by looking for solutions. But this is after you have successfully convinced yourself that the main cause of the issue is not about what has happened. But it is the aftermath of the event that is the issue. While blaming shifts the mantle of ownership and responsibility to others, self-responsibility and ownership return the power to you. The moment you are truly convinced, you have made remarkable progress then it is time to be in search of a worthy solution. It is simple to fuel and excuse the progression of an addictive attitude by accusing others. Allow yourself by acknowledging what has occurred and understanding how to survive the difficulties posed by the incident.

Task

Taking responsibility for yourself and your own well-being takes a lot of courage, but it will give you back control and a sense of freedom. Try taking the following step:

- Complaining- is always a bad habit and you need to realise and take a mental note of when you are doing it and try to limit this behaviour. Complaining about a situation or a person will automatically put you in the position of being a victim, which we are trying to avoid. You also get stuck in a rut and whilst concentrating on complaining about a situation, you fail to find a solution. On the other hand, if you spend less time and energy complaining, you'll have more time and energy to think and act on a situation.

LETTING GO OF THE PAST

Letting go of past traumatic experiences is indeed very challenging. Traumatic experiences end up leaving a big scar. If you have been affected by trauma, not only is your daily life affected, but everything that pertains to your life. Beliefs, decisions and decision-making processes are also affected. Letting go of your past traumatic experiences is not easy to achieve, but it CAN be achieved.

There are many examples of these traumatic incidents that cannot be easy to let go of. Some of these incidents include past intimate relationships and friendships, recognizable failures, mistakes, regrets and upsetting and disturbing events.

Why it is difficult to let go of the past

We all get affected by life incidents in different ways. Reactions of people differ, and that depends on a lot of factors. Some find it pretty easy to move on immediately after a traumatic incident and others do not. Some end up having a serious problem with mental health.

Most people think that trauma only happens when serious issues are invoked. They believe that it has to do with pain, anger, war etc., but this is not always the case most of the time. It might take the form of secondary vicarious trauma as well, where you are not directly affected but only close to people affected. There is also something referred to as rumination. Rumination is the process where someone thinks about an incident so much to the extent that it becomes very excessive. This is because some people have successfully adapted his method as their coping mechanism. This set of people believes that adopting rumination as a coping mechanism grants them more insight and increases their journey of recovery and self-healing.

Well, that is what they might think, but in the real sense of it, rumination only worsens the situation. It makes the self-healing process very difficult and, therefore, reduces the rate of self-healing and discovery. Rumination is a symptom common to most mental-related issues like depression, post-traumatic stress disorder, anxiety disorder and obsessive-compulsive syndrome. Rumination also encourages traumatic survivors to have a strong grip on the past, and this is very dangerous. It might not be an intentional act on the part of the survivor. It might be the survivor trying to imagine and learn from positive experiences in place of the traumatic experience that has long occurred. It might also be the survivor unconsciously. But whatever reason it is that might have made the survivors embrace this approach, only ends up drawing back the patient's rate of recovery.

Task

The following steps will assist you further in letting go of the past. It will help you move forward.

Firstly, you have to feel ready. This can happen at any time to different people. This is because it doesn't follow any rigid rules and follow a particular pattern. But once you finally realize this and make that decision, it is indeed a great step. It is such a necessary overpowering decision.

Second, do not try to evade or skip any feeling. Instead, feel it.

Answer this question to yourself: What emotional feelings does your past provoke?

While answering this question, feel all the possible emotions attached to the traumatic incident you went through or are still going through. The feelings come without control, and just let them arrive, observe, accept it without overthinking or dwelling. Feel, accept and let go.

After you have accepted how situations have made you feel it is time to let go and make a conscious decision to leave what does not serve you in the past where it belongs . How you react is what determines your role in it. This isn't the best time to start proving what is not, as long as you do not allow these emotions to determine what you will do or how you react. Memories and events are indeed really strong, but from time to time, if you allow yourself to feel these emotions, they become less powerful. This is only if you do not fight them. It might prove very difficult initially, but some ways to feel good each time is by seeing a therapist or talking with a trusted person.

Mindfulness

Being mindful is a special ability that enables you to concentrate on present challenges. This will be a great help to those who are dealing with rumination or trying to leave the past behind them. An experiment carried out in 2016 suggested people that who practice mindfulness do not experience rumination thoughts frequently compared to people who do not practice it. In addition, very mindful people are usually more compassionate to themselves compared to people who aren't and self-care is essential for the healing process to be successful. If you haven't consciously practised mindfulness before, this might be a challenging phenomenon for you. If you see this as a challenge, here are a few ways to practise mindfulness below:

Task

- Being thankful for the simple things in life; the small wins and small joys. This might include the joy of waking up. Some small joys include appreciating delicious food, etc.

- Appreciating nature and spending more time with nature

- Taking part in conscious and intelligent hobbies such as playing the pianos and other musical instruments, singing, riding, drawing.

- Taking part in concentration activities like meditation.

If you have never meditation before, you can try this approach:

- Pick a location that is quiet and with fewer distractions. If it is possible to get a place with ZERO interruptions, that will be a very good option.

- Close your eyes and start noticing your breath

- Then begin to Inhale and exhale deeply, brining your attention to your belly feeling it fill up with air then slowly being emptied.

- Continue focusing on the act of breathing and the movement of your belly. If your mind wonders and begin to have any type of thoughts, you can briefly allow it, accept, observe and let go what doesn't serve you. Always return back to your deep inhalation and exhalation concentrating on this process.

- Continue this for as long as you feel necessary

The whole concept of practising mindfulness is for the essence of feeling the present. The repetitive process of all the above points helps you to focus on the present, making you dwell less in the past. It can be helpful because it helps you visualize your thoughts. Some people might find it very helpful to repeat a process because it reminds them of the present more than the others.

Being self-compassionate has to do with treating yourself with attention, care, and sympathy. Most people do not know how to practice self-compassion because they do not see anything good about themselves. Aside from that, they are so preoccupied with focusing on their mistakes that they have forgotten how to treat themselves with forgiveness, kindness and care. There are many ways to be self-compassionate, and ways is by altering your self-talk. Be less critical of yourself and more praising.

Movement

You may underestimate exercise as a tool for your mental well-being. However, incorporating movement into your day can have many advantages regarding your mental clarity and stability, which will help you further along you path to recovery. It's no secret that physical exercise release endorphins. Our bodies use the production of endorphins to deal with stress and pain. Regular exercise has been proven to naturally boost endorphin production. A little goes a long way; getting daily exercise will not only help improve your general mood and allow you to sleep better, but will also aid the reduction of anxiety and stress, decreasing symptoms of depression. Studies have shown that daily exercise has a similar effect on the body as an antidepressant drug.

TASK

Finding motivation to exercise at the best of times it hard to do, do not worry if you are not into sports or do not enjoy exercising. The trick is to start small; studies have confirmed that a 15 minute moderate run or simply walking for an hour can have the desired effect. There is no need to spend hours of your busy day frantically training, five times a week is enough and you can spend around 30 minutes a time, depending on the type of exercise. To get the most benefit from your exercise, keep your mind from wondering and concentrate on your body and how it feels while you are exercising. Focusing on the sensations you feel whilst taking any form of exercise, will help your body move out of the classic post-trauma stress response mode.

Firstly, try to set aside the time in the day for the workout when you know your energy levels are at their highest. Set aside 15 minutes 5 times a week for a brisk walk, this should be enough to begin with to increase your mood and clear your mind. You'll slowly begin to reap the benefits and feel better, which should automatically motivate you to do a little more each time, gradually feeling more energetic and less stressed.

If, of course, you have a specific activity you love doing start with that. Anything from gardening to bike riding. The more you enjoy it, the quicker you'll see the results. There are also some small changes to you daily routine that can be made to increase the amount of movement you get in the day. Taking the stairs at work, instead of the elevator for example is a simple idea.

Don't Isolate

Suffering from trauma can cause you to disconnect from the people around you. Many people are prone to withdraw from society in general and avoid social activities. A vital part of your recovery is to stay connected, support systems are important to our well-being on a good day! This could be your neighbours, friends, colleagues, teachers or family. Social connections improve your self-esteem and decrease symptoms of depression.

Task

Start with making a point of not spending too much time alone. Make an effort to participate in social gatherings even if you don't feel like you want to, especially with those who were close to you before the traumatic event.

A great way to start connecting with people again is to offer your help. This week find someone around you that could benefit from your help. It could be walking a neighbour's dog or doing some grocery shopping for an elderly family member. This will not only help you re-connect with others, but will also make you feel less helpless and more powerful.

Chapter Six

AFTER TRAUMA; WHAT NEXT?

- Understanding the impact of trauma

- Proper management of trauma

- Dealing with stigmatization

Understanding the impact of trauma: long- and short-term responses to traumatic experiences

To properly take care of trauma cases, one has to have a wide knowledge of traumatic stress-induced reactions and the popular responses that follow suits. Health and support care providers need to be fully aware of the popular experiences trauma patients might encounter after a traumatic situation. This is because treatment of trauma isn't just a straightforward thing, as people get affected by traumas in different ways. While some may exhibit traits associated with Post Traumatic Stress Disorder, also known as PTSD, other people might show off some subtle subclinical signs and symptoms that might or might not be easily detected by medical diagnosis.

The effects can indeed be mild, average, explosive, or greatly destructive. All of which do not possess a positive inner attribute. In summary, how people react to trauma depends on quite a lot of factors. Some of these factors include the behavioural makeup of an individual, the type of occasion that led to this traumatic experience, sociocultural factors, experiences, emotional strength of such a person and how each person defines and deals with stress and trauma.

As we stated earlier, a trauma patient reacts to trauma conditions differently from another survivor. Whether it is due to their pre-experiences or other factors, the sequence of reactions largely depends on many factors. Some of these factors include the rate at which they have access to support and caregivers, individual coping mechanisms, skills and talents, plus how much care and support they get from their immediate family members. Despite that, these reactions differ in severity; most times, the IMMEDIATE RESPONSE is always a natural measure that helps to curb this trauma situation temporarily.

According to medical experts, the response to a traumatic experience is less significant than the rate at which one can cope and still maintain a sane composure long after. This means that coping with stress by being healthily involved in life activities is much more worthy to note than how people respond to trauma. Some of the life activities involve going on with your day-to-day activity without attracting too much attention from others based on your behaviour and attitude, healthily regulating your emotions in the best way possible, building and maintaining strong self-esteem and having a good interpersonal relationship with both insiders and outsiders.

Trauma can cut short your hope for the future. This can also affect your excitement and expectations about life or even make you scared about facing the future. Instead of looking forward and realising that these emotions and feelings will pass, many people tend to dwell more on the immediate and initial responses to their trauma, some of them include: exhaustion, social dissociation, long term and possibly unending confusion, physical arousal, sadness, numbness, agitation and anxiety.

When this trauma isn't attended to, it can escalate into continuous fatigue, abnormal sleeping patterns, continuous bad dreams and nightmares, distress based on fear of a recurrence and incident flashbacks, low self-esteem, emotion tampering and a strong feel of depression.

Emotional response to trauma

When talking about the emotional reactions to trauma, it can be categorically emphasized that it is mostly geared to one's personal sociocultural history. Aside from the emotional reactions during trauma cases, it is also possible that common emotional acts like shame, anger, fear and sadness are most likely to occur and be identified as the initial emotional reaction as well; they are quite common types of emotional reactions. Nonetheless, it might be a daunting task to identify these reactions as a feedback response for a trauma survivor and might not be the immediate resort reaction for most survivors. Survivors might have either gotten used to this feeling. Some even feel these reactions are really dangerous as they are labelled with different names like " running mad" or "going crazy" or "losing it", etc. So, these negative labels do not allow them to feel these emotions, instead they block the emotions and act emotionally strong.

Under emotional reactions to trauma, there is something referred to as emotional dysregulation. This is best seen in some trauma survivors who have not mastered the act of regulating their emotions. This is very common in people who have faced trauma at an early age. They find it very difficult to regulate their different emotions of shame, anger, sadness, and anxiety.

Emotional dysregulation becomes a regular long-lived phenomenon. In order to block or cope with their emotions, some people suffering from emotional dysregulation resort to substance abuse and self-medication. These substances elicit a change during use, but their effects are short-term, and they are back to their original emotional state before long. This thereby leads to maintaining that emotional state for longer. This is, of course, dangerous because contrary to what they seek, it leads to more damage and a longer period of emotional dysregulation.

Some other common acts aimed at regulating one's emotions involve taking part in self-damaging and high-risk behaviours, emotional denials, overworking, distorted eating habits, self-harm etc. However, it is best to note that not all actions aimed at self-regulation are bad or dangerous. Some of them are positive traits, termed healthy, and a good way to deal with trauma. Examples of these include setting up a survivor organization, more commitment to prayers and meditation, etc.

However, based on various research, it has been found out that traumatic stress usually leads to two different emotional extreme situations. It either leaves you emotionally overwhelmed, or it leaves you emotionally empty and numb. With the right dose of love, care and self-help, survivors can begin to live again regulate emotions appropriately. The major aim of any treatment administered is to assist the trauma survivor in perfectly learning the craft of emotional regulation without having to resort to substance use or other substance-induced behaviours that mask as a solution, but in actual sense is causing more harm than good. Here, positive coping skills are advised, and survivors are lectured on how to manage distress situations.

These coping mechanisms and recovery lectures include mental restructuring and mindfulness exercises. In addition, it might also include trauma aimed desensitization measures which include reprocessing, exposure therapy and eye gesture desensitization.

Numbing can be best described as a biological procedure that involves the detachment of emotions from one's actions, memories and thoughts. This can be best noticed in a survivor's interpersonal relationships with others and the incapability of the survivor to attach emotions and feelings to whatever led to the trauma. This isn't bad. In recent research, the importance of having numbness as an aftermath of traumatic stress has been identified and emphasized. This is because numbness helps to conceal inner emotions perfectly. Therefore, levels of trauma, stress signs and symptoms, plus the impact are less serious than they truly are.

Physical reactions to trauma

Diagnosing PTSD comes with a great emphasis on the physical symptoms of trauma. In reality, people are likely to experience or not experience physical symptoms when dealing with traumatic stress. Also, the initial stages of trauma stress are often associated with physical signs and symptoms. So often, this is usually the first resort to offer care during trauma case reports.

There is a strong connection between Adverse Childhood Experiences (ACEs) and chronic health conditions as well. Some popular physical symptoms include loss of appetite, distorted eating patterns, unusual and disturbed sleeping patterns, gastrointestinal and dermatological disorders, cardiovascular and respiratory function imbalance, plus distortion in the musculoskeletal and respiratory system functioning. Trauma patients are also likely to suffer from substance use disorders and urological problems.

The physical manifestations and symptoms of emotional stress, are referred to as "somatization". Somatization best describes the phenomenon in which there is a central focus on all the symptoms experienced by the body to express any form of emotional trauma.

Some people may not wish to explore the emotional side of their trauma but would rather report the physical complaints instead. Even when tests are carried out, and there is a lapse in the emotional aspect, they feel more comfortable reporting their ailment based on their physical manifestations. The point of emphasizing this point is that once it reaches this level, a patient would prefer to report the physical signs and symptoms, rather than the emotional side or together with the emotional side, even when it is necessary, somatization becomes a mental illness.

Advice for counsellors handling trauma survivors

- **Giving your clients a proper education**

Some trauma survivors go through trauma without realizing that some symptoms are there because they are going through traumatic stress. Lecture them about the various symptoms that might include hyperarousal, physiological responses because of extreme traumatic stress, distorted sleep, and other aligning physical stress symptoms.

- Communicate with them as regards all treatment activities.

Carrying trauma stressed patients along through all their treatment stages is a good way to improve all symptoms relating to their physiology and psychology. Some of these treatment methods include yoga, therapy sessions, exercises, and meditations. If the need arises, you can refer these people to a psychiatrist. A psychiatrist will do a thorough mental evaluation and recommend a psychotropic treatment that will help address underlying severe symptoms. But this should be done only if it is necessary.

- Open discussions

It is also advisable that you have an open discussion about all trauma symptoms, including the psychological and physiological components attached to them as a counsellor. You can also do well to do a proper explanation regarding the connection between substance use disorder and traumatic stress signs and symptoms if need be.

- Avoid making the matter seem worse

Take your time to explain to these people that trauma symptoms are normal. Making it look like a flaw or weakness signs might make the patients more damaged. It can also make them feel like they are going crazy. This is because it has the potential to distort the healing process of such a person.

- Be supportive

Support your clients as much as you can. Talk to them, give them hope, joke and laugh with them and make them feel they are not alone. While doing this, be sure always to remind them they are close to recovering from their condition.

Dealing with stigmatisation

Stigmatization is closely related to a higher PTSD risk. Stigma is the negative view or opinion towards people with perceived conditions that the society does not really consider on par with its values. Stigma is simply discrimination at best which could be about a number of issues, including the long age battle of religion, race, health issues, and sexual orientation, among others. Stigma usually stems from the need to place blame at the feet of someone, it is far easier to blame whatever issues you have on others rather than looking within yourself for the possible reason of the problem. Stigma and discrimination go hand in hand; stigma refers to how you are perceived, while discrimination means that it is not just a perception but rather actively treating someone in a terrible manner.

The World Health Organisation refers to stigma as "a mark of shame, disgrace or disapproval which results in an individual being rejected, discriminated against, and excluded from participating in several different areas of society." (2001).

Stigmatization is not age-restricted. From the young ones in kindergarten to those of more advanced ages, each one of them has a bias towards a specific matter. The stigma, which in turn leads to discrimination, is one of the leading reasons for hate crimes. The need to attach guilt to a specific group of persons for various problems you might be facing, such as the covid-19 social-stigma problem associated with Asians as the virus originated in Asia, is a good example of stigma.

Stigmatization leads to quite many problems, violence being the extreme. Stigmatization could cause people to withhold vital information that could lead to loss of life. Persons suffering from this stigma may find it scary to seek help they desperately need due to fear of society and its biased beliefs. Persons that are stigmatised may suffer from segregation, melancholy, loss of job opportunities, low self-esteem, a bleak outlook on life, loss of adequate education, decent healthcare, verbal and physical abuse that arises from discrimination due to stigma.

It is necessary to understand that the media is a potent force, and proper care should be taken that whatever makes it to our screen have great messages as media content also sways the beliefs of people, and as such, if the content of the media is negative, it can harm its viewers. The content of media must be screened meticulously to avoid teaching a mass audience bad habits.

Types of Stigma

Institutional Stigma: this type of stigma refers to government policies or privately-owned institutions that purposely or inadvertently reduce a person or a group of people's opportunities to have a better life.

Public stigma refers to the negative bias that the general public has to a particular state of affairs or life choices that a person or group of persons make.

Self-Stigma: after experiencing stigmatization from various angles for a long time, those at the receiving end of this barbaric act tend to start internalising and believing that their actions deserve the censor it receives from others.

Problems Related to Stigmatization

Ignorance: in this age of quick search engines and information at the tip of your fingers, it is sad to note that people are misinformed about the most basic things when it comes to social matters. This problem deals with a lack of knowledge. Hence, they stigmatize others without having all the necessary information to make an informed decision. Ignorance is the major reason people are stigmatized because it is human nature to fear things that we do not understand. However, times have changed, you can no longer blame your bad behaviour on ignorance, and as such, you need to study, it is not enough to be well-read in one field, extend your horizon, study the plights of the minority, try to see what you can do to help the fight against stigmatization in your little way.

Prejudice: this also stems from ignorance; it is a problem with people's attitudes. It is a bias formed from not having sufficient knowledge about a state of things. This bias generally colours your interaction with everyone you come in contact with. Prejudice can be cultivated from childhood; a child may have been taught that a minority group was inferior. This prejudice follows the child into adulthood and shows in their behaviour. At times, prejudices may be cultivated out of fear or lack of understanding of the unknown. You can no longer place people in boxes you consider normal and an unrelenting stubbornness not to change with the times. Most times, this bias leads to violence and hostile relations among the groups.

Discrimination: This problem relates with how people act when faced with things they do not fully grasp. This is the last step in the pyramid that is stigmatization, the stigmatized end up being discriminated against for things that they have no control over in most cases. Discrimination may come in different facets, including being cut off from decent healthcare, loss of benefits at work, loss of good education and job opportunities, physical and verbal abuse, social isolation, problems finding accommodations etc.

These three problems must all be addressed simultaneously because dealing with one does not guarantee that the stigmatization will end.

Elements of Stigma

Perceptions of weakness: the belief that a person is weak if they do not fit your standard of a strong person or what that person can withstand. The belief that members of the male gender are predominantly strong and must not show any sign of weakness, such as suffering from depression or receiving counselling, is a good example of this.

Perceptions of being dangerous: this is predominantly thought about in relation to persons with mental illness. It is perceived that if someone has mental illness, they are expected to display violent tendencies.

Perceptions of a person's self-control: this mostly relates to mental illness matters but can also apply to the LGBTQIA community; they believe that they can control their illness or who they for in love with, as the case may be.

Shame and Guilt: this simply says that it is not fear or angst of what society has to say about your issue, but that the person is ashamed of their situation. For instance, depression, or that they feel guilty for feeling that way.

Social distance: in this instance, a person begins to distance themselves after suffering from one form of trauma or the other because their friends and relations have begun to distance themselves from them or they fear them or do not know how to relate with their friend after the traumatic experience they underwent.

Ways to Improve the Society's Reaction to Stigma

- The records of those seeking help with their health should be kept confidential in various communities.

- By providing the general community with correct information to avoid unnecessary discrimination due to ignorance of the necessary facts, people generally fear what they cannot properly understand.

- Speaking up on matters of much controversy and speaking up on any negative action by the government and marking it out as inhumane.

- Conducting the necessary research to know where help is most needed to help in curbing stigmatization.

- Using every available outlet, including television, radio to let people know that stigmatization is not an act the community condones. Also, ensuring that the media is dead-on with its representation of people being stigmatized.

- Knowing the reach of social media and adequately putting it to use in creating and increasing awareness of stigmatization and finding a way to use it to share the story of people's experience with stigmatization.

- Every individual also has a role to play in preventing stigmatization. You need to get yourself outside your comfort zone, read about the challenges that other communities are experiences, learn to relate with these experiences, and in turn, you will realise that you are becoming self-conscious and realise that some statements you make for fun or which you might regard as slang is derogatory.

- Learn to correct people around you when they are making inaccurate statements in a polite manner.

- Do not identify a person as an illness, but rather identify the person as someone suffering from an illness. Consider saying that five has Autism and not that five is autistic, note that your language is very important, for words can be quite cutting when used improperly.

- Endeavour not to be narrow-minded. Avoid placing people in checkboxes and understand that the world has gone beyond stereotypes and checking boxes and that everyone is unique in their own way. We should be canvassing for inclusivity rather than discriminating against those we feel do not conform to society's standards.

- Awareness campaigns are necessary. It has been shown that if two or more persons suffering from a stigma come out and shed light on their plights, it has a favourable effect on society. A survey carried out in 2020 showed that many adolescents and young adults showing signs of depression searched online by accessing the stories of others who have experienced depression at one time.

- Be self-aware, show empathy for those experiencing stigma and as such, those around you will follow suit.

Ways of Dealing with Stigmatization

Avoid Isolating Yourself: people experiencing stigmatization for one reason, either mental illness, sexually transmitted infections, or even their sexual orientation and who have experienced nothing but torture due to their issues may be resistant to reaching out to anyone for help. However, this should not be the case as no man can be an island. You need and deserve support while undergoing treatment or just someone to be there while going through life-altering changes in your life or body. Do not close yourself off, instead reach out and give your loved ones the chance to surround you with their love and support.

Support Groups: do not adopt the mindset that you can fight your battles yourself. It is enough to be strong because trust me, there will be days when you literally feel like you cannot go on, and you will need someone to catch you. Being a part of a support group does not make you weak; it goes to show how courageous you are by admitting that you cannot fight this battle on your own. Support groups provide you with the opportunity to meet people experiencing what you are facing, those who overcame their struggles and those still in it alongside you. It allows you to gain strength from knowing you are not alone and that some really understand your pain. It gives you the opportunity to have a sponsor or mentor who will act as an anchor for you. Check your locality for available support groups; attend a few meetings of several support groups to know which will be the right fit for you.

Speak out and Protest: it is not enough to suffer in silence; speak out. Take every opportunity to shed light on the issues you have or those prevailing in your community. Your solemn duty is to speak out for what you believe in and give voice to those who, like you, have decided to stick to the shadows. You don't need to make a big publication. Baby steps are good. You can start with your immediate family, walk up to your friends than those outside your friend circle and on and on until your message becomes a sort of gospel. Also, protests can be carried out where the civil rights of individuals are being infringed upon. Speaking out and advocating is like a call to arms by creating awareness about stigmatization in our society and its adverse effects. It also gets the community talking about matters that are generally regarded as under the table issues or matters that are never spoken about, taking the LGBTQIA community, for example.

Undergoing Treatment: Realising that you have a problem is a big step, but you also need to go out there and get the treatment you need. You may decide to keep your illness to yourself instead of seeking help to avoid being stigmatized. However, you cannot allow fear of being stigmatized not allow you to seek the help you need to help you live the quality of life you can live with much-needed treatment; this is especially the case for people with mental illness or those suffering from sexually transmitted infections.

Contact: it is believed that having no contact with those experiencing stigmatization leads to increased fear, gives people misgivings and unsettles them (Cook et al., 2014). In essence, fostering contact between the stigmatized and the masses helps bridge the gap and foster better understanding and relationships. This contact-based method is a way of decreasing public stigma.

Be Positive: be positive and not think bad thoughts. You should not think of yourself as someone that should be stigmatized because you feel you are an illness or a disease. You must learn to differentiate between yourself and the illness and know that nothing you are experiencing makes you worthy of being stigmatized.

Seek Help at School: for the little ones, if you are experiencing any form of stigmatization at school and you have been made the brunt of a lot of jokes due to a learning disability or whatever reason, you need to seek help within your school. Look for a trusted teacher or lecturer to help you and not keep everything bottled up inside. This is not limited to little children but also extends to university students also.

Avoid Self-Doubt: in dealing with stigmatization, you need to wire your thoughts and align your thoughts positively. Even if you are being discriminated against due to one prejudice or the other, you must never look at yourself as the cause. Nothing you have done or are experiencing gives anybody any right to make you feel wrong or to blame. You must build your self-worth. You must believe in your worthiness and have no shame regarding what you are enduring, but consider yourself a fighter who will triumph over all odds.

Know Your Rights Under the Law: the law protects its citizens, although these protections are not all comprehensive and still need some work in cases where no provisions protect your right. However, know what rights are available to you and use them when necessary to protect yourself from harm.

Counselling: Everyone copes differently with problems in their own unique way, some people can decide to work it out all on their own, and most times, they are successful, and some of us need help from a professional. There is absolutely nothing wrong with going to counselling sessions if you feel you might need them.

Challenge Gender-Based Stereotypes: there are biases targeted toward different gender; take the initiative to challenge these stereotypes that believe only a particular gender can experience some things and that the other gender may be considered weak if they experience the same thing.

In conclusion, stigmatization is a big problem that has plagued our society for ages and the fight to stop stigmatization has been ongoing for quite a long time. However, it is not a single person's battle; it is something we should all strive for in our own little corners of the world; no more "it is not my business", it is time we all take a stand and say NO TO STIGMATIZATION.

CONCLUSION:

TOTAL RECOVERY FROM TRAUMA

ACCOMPLISHING RECOVERY

Recovery is achieved by going through these stages listed above. It takes time and you must be patient. You will gradually see the signs of change and recovery every day until you achieve a total and final recovery. When you are not being affected by the emotional pain of the traumatic event anymore, you easily view your traumatic experience from a healthy view point and successfully get past this event with no feeling that the trauma experience is still controlling you.

Summary

Trauma Symptoms, Causes and Effects

Trauma is characterized by the American Psychological Association (APA) as the enthusiastic reaction somebody has to a very adverse occasion. While the trauma is an ordinary response to a horrendous occasion, the impacts can be excessively extreme to where they meddle with a singular's capacity to carry on with a typical life. For a situation like this, help might be expected to treat the pressure and brokenness brought about by the awful accident and re-establishes the person to a condition of passionate prosperity.

What Are the Main Sources of Trauma?

Trauma can be brought about by a predominantly adverse occasion that causes an enduring effect on the casualty's psychological and enthusiastic dependability. While many wellsprings of trauma are fierce, others are mental. Some normal wellsprings of trauma include:

- Assault

- Aggressive behaviour at home

- Cataclysmic events

- Extreme ailment or trauma

- The demise of a friend or family member

- Seeing a demonstration of brutality

What Are the Signs of a Person Suffering from Trauma?

While the causes and side effects of trauma are different, there are some essential indications of trauma that you can pay special mind to. Individuals who have experienced trauma will regularly seem shaken and bewildered. They may not react to the discussion as they ordinarily would have and will regularly seem removed or not present when talking.

One more sign of a trauma casualty is nervousness. Uneasiness because of trauma can show in issues like night fear, restlessness, helpless focus and emotional episodes. While these manifestations of trauma are normal, they are not comprehensive. People react to trauma in various ways. Now and again, trauma is practically unnoticeable even to the casualty's dearest companions and family. These cases represent the significance of conversing with somebody after an awful accident has happened, regardless of whether they give no underlying indications of unsettling reactions. Signs of trauma can show up days, months or even a very long time after the genuine occasion.

Enthusiastic Symptoms of Trauma

Some normal enthusiastic manifestations of trauma incorporate refusal, outrage, bitterness and passionate upheavals. Survivors of trauma might divert the staggering feelings they experience toward different sources, like companions or relatives. This is one reason the trauma is hard for friends and family as well. It is difficult to help somebody who drives you away, yet understanding the enthusiastic side effects of a horrendous mishap can facilitate the interaction.

The present moment and Long-Term Effects of Trauma

All trauma impacts can occur either throughout a brief timeframe or throughout weeks, or even a long time. Any impacts of trauma ought to be addressed promptly to forestall lastingness. The sooner the trauma is tended to, the better possibility a casualty has of recuperating effectively and completely.

Trauma Medication: Drug Options

While trauma, in contrast to some other mental problems, is started by an occasion or experience, it very well may be treated using certain drugs. Not all traumas require a prescription, but it is a helpful instrument in treating the manifestations of trauma, like nervousness and despair. Work with medical services proficient to decide if the prescription is vital.

Medication choices will rely upon the person's mental and clinical history, just as the seriousness of the manifestations. If sorrow is serious and felt throughout a lengthy timeframe, it could be treated with normal stimulant medications. Clinical discouragement is characterized as any burdensome scene enduring longer than 90 days. Many trauma casualties fall under the class of nervousness victims who are qualified for hostility to tension medicine.

Prescription Side Effects

One contemplates on whether the cure for the manifestations of trauma has drug incidental effects. All prescriptions have incidental effects, and the seriousness differs depending on drug class and individual body science. Some incidental effects are more sensitive than others, and potential negative incidental effects should consistently be contrasted with the expected advantage to the patient.

Medicine Overdose

Medicine glut happens when somebody ingests a critical enough measure of the drug to cause actual damage. Excess frequently happens related to substance misuse; however, it very well might be inadvertent and happen under customary conditions. Any example of excess ought to be treated seriously, and expert help ought to be looked at to guarantee that excess doesn't reoccur and to decide whether the reason is substance misuse.

Double Diagnosis: Addiction and Trauma

When the indications of PTSD, melancholy and tension become a lot to adapt to through ordinary means, many casualties of trauma go to substance misuse. As referenced, casualties are substantially more liable to foster addictions than different individuals from everyone. It is fundamental for the friends and family of trauma victims to pay special attention to the indications of fixation after trauma, regardless of whether the enslavement is the main outward sign of PTSD.

Finding support for Trauma-Related Issues

If you or a friend or family member is experiencing trauma, there is help accessible. With an assortment of trauma treatment choices and caring experts willing to help.

Nothing lasts forever

CPSIA information can be obtained
at www.ICGtesting.com
Printed in the USA
LVHW061101130222
711034LV00007B/498